Sámi Artists

Monica L. Edmondson
Per Enoksson
Sune Enoksson
Bente Geving
Josef Halse
Marja Helander
Arnold Johansen
Annelise Josefsen
Per Isak Juuso
Johanne Losoa Larsson
Max Lundström
Britta Marakatt Labba
Hege Annestad Nilsen
Hilde Skancke Pedersen
Inga Nordsletta Pedersen
Synnøve Persen
Outi Pieski
Alf Magne Salo
Iria Čiekča Schmidt
Ingunn Utsi
Nils Arvid Westerfjell

In the Shadow of the Midnight Sun

Sámi and Inuit Art 2000-2005

Art Gallery of Hamilton

engage your imagination

Library and Archives Canada Cataloguing in Publication

Art Gallery of Hamilton
Blodgett, Jean - 1945
In the Shadow of the Midnight Sun: Sámi and Inuit Art 2000-2005 / Jean Blodgett.
Translation from Norwegian to English by Eileen Fredriksen

Publication in conjunction with the travelling exhibition of contemporary Sámi and Inuit art of the same name, first held at the Art Gallery of Hamilton, 14 January – 7 May 2006 and travelling to:

The Rooms, St. John's, Newfoundland – 16 February – 20 April 2007
The Winnipeg Art Gallery, Winnipeg, Manitoba – 19 May – 19 August 2007
Yukon Arts Centre, Whitehorse, Yukon Territory – 10 January – 9 March 2008
National Gallery of Canada, Ottawa, Ontario – 23 May – 17 August 2008
Includes bibliographical references.

ISBN 0-919153-86-0   978-0-919153-86-08

1. Art, Sámi – exhibitions 2. Art, Inuit - exhibitions
3. Art, Modern – 21st century – exhibitions 4. Art Gallery of Hamilton
I Blodgett, Jean – 1945 II. Title

N6549.5.I58B56 2006   704.0397107471352   C2006-901920-7

Distributed by:
ABC Art Books Canada Distribution
www.ABCartbookscanada.com

Printed in Canada by Kromar Printing Ltd., Winnipeg
Design: factor[e] design initiative
Installation photos: Robert McNair
Artwork photos: Roy Timm

TABLE OF CONTENTS

123 King St. West
Hamilton, Ontario
L8P 4S8
905 527 6610
www.artgalleryofhamilton.com

This exhibition was organized and circulated by the Art Gallery of Hamilton. This project has been made possible in part through a contribution from the Museums Assistance Program, Department of Canadian Heritage.

 Canadian Heritage   Patrimoine canadien

The Art Gallery of Hamilton wishes to thank the City of Hamilton, its members and friends. As well, it is grateful for the generous assistance of the Canada Council for the Arts and the Ontario Arts Council.

 Canada Council for the Arts   Conseil des Arts du Canada   ONTARIO ARTS COUNCIL CONSEIL DES ARTS DE L'ONTARIO   Hamilton

FOREWORD

In the Shadow of the Midnight Sun: Sámi and Inuit Art 2000-2005 is one of the Art Gallery of Hamilton's most dynamic projects presenting a unique and revealing selection of art being produced by Inuit and Sámi artists today. This is the first exhibition of its kind that has attempted to investigate the work of these two cultural groups together. Since its conception four years ago, **In the Shadow of the Midnight Sun** has been envisioned as an exhibition that would identify cultural threads of connection that unite and distinguish the art of the Canadian Inuit and Scandinavian Sámi. The exhibition reflects on the shared social, historical and topographical conditions that influence the work of these artists. The endeavour, undertaken by Guest Curator and expert in Canadian Inuit art, Jean Blodgett, is a *tour de force*, resulting in an exquisite project that showcases a diverse selection of works including prints, sculptures, paintings, wall hangings, drawings and photographs.

After its showcase in Hamilton, the exhibition is scheduled to tour to The Rooms, St. John's, Newfoundland; The Winnipeg Art Gallery, Manitoba; the Yukon Arts Centre in Whitehorse, Yukon Territory; and the National Gallery of Canada in Ottawa, Ontario. Following the Canadian tour, it will grace the spaces of several museums in Scandinavia.

In the Shadow of the Midnight Sun has been a lengthy and complex undertaking and as with any project of this scale, many people and organizations have played a key role in its success and deserve to be acknowledged. We are grateful to the Curator of the exhibition, Jean Blodgett for her intensive research and the energy she put into the project. We also would like to thank Irene Snarby, Curator at the Sámi Museum in Karasjok for her help in securing Sámi artworks and Pat Feheley for bringing the idea of this exhibition to our attention. We are extremely grateful to the lenders to this exhibition, public and private collectors, who have entrusted us with works from their collections and generously agreed to part with them for a substantial period of time so that they can be shared with a larger public.

I would also like to thank the Canada Council for the Arts, the Ontario Arts Council, and the City of Hamilton, its members and friends for their ongoing support of our programmes. A special note of thanks to The Department of Foreign Affairs and International Trade, Canada, the Royal Norwegian Embassy, Ottawa, the Embassy of Sweden, Ottawa, the Canadian Embassies in Norway, Sweden, Finland and Denmark for their financial assistance in supporting the Scandinavian touring component of the project.

Thank you to the AGH staff whose dedication and work at all levels contribute to making our projects a success. Thank you to the Board of Directors and Council of Governors for their ongoing support.

Finally, thank you to all the artists who participated in the exhibition giving us much to discover and think about.

Louise Dompierre
President and C.E.O.

INTRODUCTION

This exhibition had its genesis in 2001 as a cultural component of the 2002 visit of Norway's King Harald V and Queen Sonja to Canada. The display was intended to show examples of visual arts made by indigenous cultures of each country: the Norwegian Sámi (previously referred to as Laplanders) and the Canadian Inuit (previously referred to as Eskimos). The exhibition could not be organized before the royal visit and therefore did not occur.

The idea for such an exhibition, however, was not forgotten and was eventually undertaken by the Art Gallery of Hamilton. Originally we kept the concept of showcasing Norwegian Sámi and Canadian Inuit art, but circumstances and events on my own trip to Norway in early 2005 made it clear that the Sámi culture is not bound by international borders. Sápmi, or the land of the Sámi, is contiguous across four different countries, extending from central to northern Norway, through upper Sweden and Finland into the most northwestern part of Russia. Sámi artists in Sweden, Finland and Norway – and their art – regularly travel back and forth across these borders; for example, the Health Center in Kautokeino, Norway has several commissioned works by Folke Fjällström, a Sámi artist from Sweden. Consequently, it was decided to extend the content of the exhibition to include work by Sámi artists in Finland and Sweden as well.

In an effort to give the exhibition a unifying concept I decided to limit the artwork to objects made between 2000 and 2005. Originally this time frame resulted from my desire to show what was happening right now in Inuit art* rather than assemble another historically based presentation or give a condensed version of the history of Sámi and Inuit art. Limiting the time period worked well with both cultures and helped focus the selection of artworks. As a way of introduction, Irene Snarby discusses not only contemporary Sámi art, but also provides an historical overview.

The title of this exhibition, In the Shadow of the Midnight Sun, is taken from a book of contemporary Sámi prose and poetry edited by Harald Gaski (Karasjok: Davvi Girji, 1996). This poetic phrase emphasizes the distance that separates the Inuit and Sámi from the more populated areas to the south. They are far enough away, in their land of the midnight sun, to retain an element of romantic exoticness for many people. With this exhibition we hope to throw some light on at least one aspect of their recent lives – the art.

Jean Blodgett
Guest Curator

---

*Christine Lalonde of the National Gallery of Canada, with the same intention, recently produced a travelling exhibition called *Inuit Sculpture Now*. Lalonde's essay in the accompanying publication was invaluable to me in my own research.

Comparing and contrasting Inuit and Sámi art

The intention of this exhibition was to present recent work by Sámi and Inuit artists; not necessarily to make comparisons between the two. However, their juxtaposition—purposely displayed side by side in the exhibition—invites at least an attempt at comparison. And sometimes such comparisons reveal heretofore unseen or unrecognized characteristics in common. The following discussion includes art from both cultures but with an emphasis on Inuit, since Sámi art is covered more extensively in the accompanying essay by Irene Snarby of De Samiske Samlinger (Sámi Museum) in Karasjok, Norway.

Although there is no evidence that the Sámi and Inuit are in any way related, they are both indigenous peoples who originally inhabited the lands now incorporated within the confines of contemporary nations; they are both a minority group that was overtaken by a majority. With the exception that Sámi contact with Europeans was earlier and more intense, their post-contact experiences have been similar in their effect on religion, language, lifestyle, learning and politics.

However, while both cultures have a long history of making specially crafted objects for functional and religious use, Inuit art has received much more concentrated attention and international interest since the 1950s. It has also received an unprecedented amount of government assistance—to a degree unknown by the Sámi.

The only time that Sámi and Inuit arts have been shown together seems to have been in the early 1990s when both were included, along with the work of indigenous people of Alaska, Greenland and Russia, in the international exhibition **Arts of the Arctic** (Sámi Artists' Union n.d.).

The most obvious difference between the art made by Sámi and Inuit artists in this exhibition is of scale and format. A number of the Sámi artists, especially the painters, work on a scale much larger than that of Inuit drawings, prints or paintings. Other Sámi artists work in a series format, building up a display of substantial scope by the repetition of a particular theme in photographs or paintings. The only Inuit artworks that can compete with the visual impact of these larger works are the bigger wall hangings made by the Baker Lake seamstresses, such as those by Janet Nungnik and Annie Taipanak in this exhibition. Other Inuit art in the exhibition ranges in size from tiny, perfectly formed ivory and stone sculptures by Silas Kayakjuak, to Abraham Anghik Ruben's large whalebone piece, *Kittigazuit*.

Several Sámi works in the exhibition can be compared with Inuit works on the simple basis of media used. Both Sámi and Inuit women have adapted their sewing skills from making clothing to creating colourful wall mounted textiles and wall hangings. Both Janet Kigusiuq (Inuit) and Iria Čiekča Schmidt (Sámi) work in paper collage while Annelise Josefsen (Sámi) works in stone like so many Inuit sculptors. Nevertheless, in spite of the common media, it is not difficult to distinguish the Inuit work from that of the Sámi. This distinction may be a matter of content, such as the Sámi clothing in Inga Nordslette Pedersen's (Sámi) work, the reindeer in Britta Marakatt-Labba's (Sámi) textile, or the symbols in Schmidt's collage.

It is primarily sculptural form rather than subject matter, that distinguishes the work of Annelise Josefsen. Both the style of the vertical component of the sculpture, with its rough, abstracted, elongated human shape with minimal details to help identify the subject and the style of the reclining Rubenesque figure are unlike those used by Inuit artists. In general, Inuit artists may carve abstracted or elongated forms; they may not smooth the stone surface of their work; or they may omit identifying elements, but they rarely, if ever, would combine all these characteristics in one sculpture. That is, in Inuit art, the abstracted or elongated form will have a polished surface or some element that identifies it with the real world while the roughly finished works tend to have only a vaguely identifiable subject matter.

Annie Pootoogook, like several other Sámi and Inuit artists in the exhibition, looks at issues of identity; self, place within Inuit culture, and Inuit culture in a wider context. She may show herself or events from her life, such as *In My Bedroom* or *Memory of My Life: Breaking Bottles* (not in exhibition).

To convey a sense of duality, Arnold Johansen's technique of utilizing accordian folded paper is ideal. By transfering two photographs to either side of the folds, the viewer is able to see a different image depending on the angle at which the work is approached.

In some instances, symbolism and ulterior meanings are employed by Sámi artists. The colours in Alf Magne Salo's painting *Apsis 3*, reflect those in Sámi clothing. In Per Enoksson's work *Sweet Brother, Stupid Sister*, big brother (Sweden) and stupid sister (Norway) represent the good-natured rivalry between Norwegians and Swedes. Monica Edmondson, for her part, explains her choice of colours in *Ellipse II* (email to the author, October 8, 2005): "the intense colours originating from my Sámi costume [are] in the center—to represent the heart and fire of life—within a plane of coldworked and etched "wintery white" (glass)."

In contrast, Inuit works of art tend to be quite literal. People, animals, events, places and activities are represented in varying degrees of realism, and while they may be more or less expressive, are generally not symbolic. Even such representations as the sea goddess Sedna, shamans, spirits or transformed beings are not symbolic or imaginary so much as they illustrate long-held beliefs—even though they may no longer exist—in shamanism and the supernatural.

Palaya Qiatsuq, whose *Sedna* is included in this exhibition, explained why he chooses certain subject matter (Fox 2001):

> When I do transformation or shamanism carvings, [I hope] the younger people will see the carving in a book or in a gallery. I want them to know that these traditions have to be carried out. They have to know that our ancestors had a hard time to live, to hunt. Sometimes they were starving. These carvings are important to me and I want to show these younger people—and others—that this happened before.

Most Sámi artists included in this exhibition are working in the style and media of contemporary international art: painting with oil and acrylic on canvas, making glass work, creating large-scale sculpture, doing photographic series, using special photographic processes, or combining media such as photography and painting. One would be hard pressed to identify a "Sámi art style" from this disparate group of works (Sámi handicrafts [*duodji*] are another matter).

In direct contrast, Inuit art has a distinctive style all its own. Like so much contemporary Inuit art, the pieces in this exhibition form a recognizable "school" or identifying characteristics of work from a particular community. Aside from some experimentation with media and subject, larger size and increased technical skills, Inuit sculpture, drawings, and prints made today look much as they did fifty years ago.

Inuit Artists Featured in the Exhibition

This consistent appearance of Inuit art though, has more to do with the form, shape and media used, than with the subject matter. While recent works by Jutai Toonoo and Annie Pootoogook may "look" like Inuit art, their subject matter is anything but "traditional" as evidenced by recent sculptures by Jutai such as *Gargoyle, New and Improved Fertility God, Woe Unto You When Your Wife Turns 40* or drawings by Annie Pootoogook such as *Busted, Watching Jerry Springer, Work Interrupted by a Phone Call, Cleaning Up in the Kitchen* or *Getting Ready for a Date*. In her drawing, *Watching Seal Hunting on Television*, we move far from the old style carving of the "hunter at a seal hole" to seal hunting as a televised spectator sport (none included in exhibition).

Both Sámi and Inuit artists may reference their homeland in their work by depicting landscape or indigenous plant and animal life. Witness the subtle signs of nature in Hilde Skancke Pedersen's (Sámi) series *Livstegn* [Sign of Life] and in Bente Geving's (Sámi) photographs or the ingenious rendering of Arctic grass and the sensitive evening landscape in the two works by Arnaqu Ashevak. Janet Kigusiuq, whose earliest drawings were realistic scenes of animals and people rendered in minute detail over the entire surface of the paper, turned more and more to landscape in her later years. Using broad washes of colour and shape and sometimes a few small details, such as pebbles, she depicted the land and water around her, often identifying the specific locale as one where she had been. Nick Sikkuark, in *Imagining Things*, investigates images hidden in the landscape and in another drawing inventively shows fragments of a landscape seen as though through holes made in the paper surface.

Arctic animals, in particular, continue to be popular in Inuit art, and artists like Kananginak Pootoogook continue to find new ways to approach this subject. Kananginak, who has been involved with the printmaking program in Cape Dorset since its inception, is particularly well known for his exquisitely detailed depictions of wildlife, especially birds. In recent years, he has posed his animal subjects in positions that are more complex and difficult to translate onto a two-dimensional surface, as seen in caribou portrayed head-on in the print, *Amiraijaqtuq: Shedding the Velvet*, included here.

Kananginak has also taken to documenting the appearance of outsiders in the Arctic—usually with a certain irony and sense of humour. Since his 1992 print, *The First Tourist*, in which a crouching non-Inuit man with a camera in one hand poses a young Inuk girl in front of an inukshuk—the quintessential Inuit symbol of built-up rocks—and holds his other hand up in the position of "hold it right there", he has continued to illustrate these visitors to his community as they tape record throat singing, photograph carvers and film drum dancing.

Isaci Etidloie has great respect for his grandparents' generation, explaining to Christine Lalonde (2005) that they had "bigger ideas than we do today because they'd heard more stories. People would tell more stories back then. Nobody hardly tells any stories any more". Isaci's work in this exhibition is based on an episode from an old story told in a new film: his *Shaman from the Story of Atanarjuat* was made after viewing a video of the now-famous Inuit film, *Atanarjuat (The Fast Runner)*, that he had rented from his local store.

The younger Inuit artists' search for subject matter relevant to them leads them away from the land, animals and spirits of previous generations. Jamasie Pudloo Pitseolak of Cape Dorset specializes in the minutiae of a settlement life that includes television and video, carving finely detailed items such as an electric guitar, the belongings of a pirate or *Domestic Sewing Machine* included in this exhibition. Sometimes the inventive artist isn't young: Anirnik Ragee, in her sixties but a newcomer to the print studios, wrote, directly on the lithographic stone, random words with the syllabic symbols used in writing the Inuktitut language, to create an intricate and colorful array of tiny elements in her 2004 print, *Field of Verse*.

Shuvinai Ashoona also shows us elements of life in Cape Dorset, but these, like most of her drawings, are a reality as seen only through her own eyes. The carefully delineated church interior is inspired by the Anglican church in Cape Dorset, while the print *Low Tide* shows ships from different time periods--both real and imagined--all pulled up onto the beach, even though the shore water in front of Cape Dorset is so shallow that ships must anchor much farther out. The **Nascopie**, which foundered just off shore from Cape Dorset in 1947, is shown together with the **Lady Franklin**, a cargo ship that operated in the Canadian Arctic in the 1980s. Next to them is a ship called **Nunavut, NWT**; a strange combination since Nunavut and NWT are two different territories in the Canadian Arctic. In fact, Nunavut came into being in 1999 when the eastern part of the Northwest Territories was separated to make this new entity. In this image, then, Shuvinai assembles two ships with recognizable names from different time periods with another ship of dubious heritage; all lined up on the unnavigable shore of Cape Dorset.

Annie Pootoogook (the daughter of Napachie Pootoogook whose print *Winsome Travellers* is included in this exhibition), has in recent years become the foremost chronicler of life in Cape Dorset. In her drawings she has captured virtually every aspect of settlement life, from substance abuse to the new ATM at the Co-op store. Included in this exhibition are two drawings that show us how old traditions are still mixed with the new. In *Christmas Games at the Community Hall*, people are dressed in a combination of old and new style clothing while they watch or play Inuit games and eat junk food from the hall's concession stand. In *Playing Super Nintendo*, we see two children in their typical northern style pre-fab house playing the now universal game of Nintendo.

Abraham Anghik Ruben records Inuit history of personal relevance from his area of the western Arctic with the sculpture *Kittigazuit*, as explained by Darlene Wight (2001):

> Kittigazuit was once a large and flourishing settlement located on the ocean coastline southwest of Tuktoyaktuk in the Mackenzie Delta area. It flourished in the 19th century because of plentiful fishing, whaling and hunting. However, a series of epidemics of scarlet fever, measles, and influenza from 1865 to 1902 killed many of its inhabitants, including members of the artist's family. Survivors left the community and dispersed along the coastline, and today it is little more than a landmark on the tundra.
>
> *Kittigazuit* is made from an ancient piece of whalebone that was part of the skull of a bowhead whale. At the base of the carving, there are a number of human faces that have no eyes, symbolizing the people who died in an epidemic. They are roughly carved in the porous bone to give a sense of history, indicating that this happened a long time ago. The sculpture has animals clustered around it: loons, seals, ravens, and bears. A raven's head beside the full moon signifies that, unlike the people, the animals continued on. There is an open space in the skull, signifying an empty land where people used to live. A woman's amautik [parka] is empty of children, just as the land is empty of people.
>
> Not only a generation, but also a culture has been lost, as Mackenzie Inuit culture changed with the arrival of many people from Alaska.

Floyd Kuptana's *Patriotic Shaman* identifies himself with Canada as he waves a maple-leaf flag. Although this sculpture reflects the carving style of his cousin David Ruben Piqtoukun, with whom he has worked, Kuptana's other piece in this exhibition, *Abductor of Souls*, certainly lives up to his stated goal (McLeod 2002): *I try to be alone and create work that is different, my own, something new.* In this sculpture he gives the hideous old woman—who in traditional tales steals the souls of misbehaving children—a modern makeover (although he doesn't seem to have improved her looks): she wears a top with a kangaroo pouch in front, useful for carrying souls and other items, a scarf like Snoopy's, and a cape, defined by the markings on her back, like a cartoon superhero. Blissfully unaware of the observer's probable reaction to her buck teeth and bulging eyes, she combs her hair—a lot of which seems to be coming out in her comb—and gazes intently into her cosmetic mirror.

Several Inuit artists demonstrate their awareness of current world events: Kavavow Mannomee's drawings show an airplane flying into the World Trade Center towers; he has also constructed a beautiful and complex sculpture of the same horrific subject, as well as a drawing commemorating the space shuttle *Challenger* disaster. Jutai Toonoo's sculpture *Censored Woman* was inspired by seeing Muslim women "who were all covered up" on television, while one of Annie Pootoogook's drawings shows Inuit *Watching the Iraqi War on T.V.* (none included in this exhibition).

Arnaqu Ashevak's delicate and intricate sculpture *Memorial* included here combines recognition of local and international tragedies. As he explains (Feheley Fine Arts 2004):

> It's symbolic, like a memorial. Up here, sometimes people get lost out on the land and are never found. This is for the people who look for them—the rescue people—and the ones who are lost. I was thinking about those twin towers in New York and how they have a memorial for them. The flower is to remember the people, and the kudlik [oil lamp] is a traditional thing that was very useful for the family up north.

Another drawing by Annie Pootoogook, *Three Generations of Women Artists*, illustrates her awareness of her place as a younger member of a talented artistic family. In order of sequence, from top to bottom, she presents the drawing style, subject matter and signature of her famous grandmother, Pitseolak Ashoona, her mother Napachie Pootoogook, another well-known Cape Dorset artist, and then herself.

Also presented, the Baker Lake wall hanging *I Love Summer* has actually been made by a mother/daughter team: Eva Ikinilik Nagyougalik and her daughter Sophie Kuutsiq Nagyougalik. Both artists have signed the back of the hanging and Sophie's name appears on the front inside a heart, giving the work the feel of a 19th-century sampler young girls made to practice their sewing skills.

Eva Ikinilik Nagyougalik, a prominent maker of wall hangings, is the biological daughter of Ruth Qaulluaryuk and Josiah Nuilaalik, a well-known sculptor and son of Baker Lake's artistic genius Jessie Oonark. She was raised, however, by two other important Baker Lake artists: Marion Tuu'luq, famous for her wall hangings, and Luke Anguhadluq, famous for his prints and drawings.

Oviloo Tunnillie is generally considered to be the first Inuit artist who has consistently presented herself as a subject in her work. Earlier artists did occasionally portray themselves, but none to the degree that Oviloo has: she has shown herself in various poses and in a number of autobiographical situations, revealing her memories and emotions. She explained to Sue Gustavison (1999: 68): "Back in the 1980s, I was asking myself, "How will I make art?" It didn't make sense to me to carve scenes of traditional life because I was not there so I began to carve from my own experiences—both happy and sad." In this exhibition, a poignant self-portrait and a portrait of herself and her daughter Tye are included. In the latter, the two women hold up a photograph taken of them in 1990 when Tye was a baby: the "photograph" is carved out of the same stone as the figures themselves.

Oviloo's brother Jutai Toonoo, mentioned previously, also often takes himself and his own situations as subject matter, but the work included by him here is a portrait of the famous Cape Dorset sculptor Osuitok Ipeelee – obviously prompted by Jutai's shock at seeing how the once great hunter had become an old man. In the sculpture an erect hunter views the world through his arctic snow goggles. Jutai explains (Feheley Fine Arts 2002b): "I was at camp with Osuitok and he wasn't the same man I used to know. This is an image of what he used to be. He was a great man; he still is."

In Inuit art, these portraits, whether of self or others, are only generalized representations of human beings; they do not show enough detail to identify the actual person depicted. It is the artist who identifies whom they have represented; for such an identification would not be possible for the viewer simply by looking at the features of the face in the sculpture or drawing.

There are two Inuit works in this exhibition that do have symbolic or referential content—interestingly both in connection with the *kudlik* or *qulliq* (oil lamp) so crucial to life in the north during traditional times. Arnaqu Ashevak 's *Memorial* (previously discussed) includes a flower and *kudlik*, and is described by him as symbolic.

In Mattiusi Iyaituk's, *Old Qulliq Being Carried by a Woman*, the old kudlik that the woman is carrying becomes her body in a very successful visual pun, at the same time it is making a special connection between the oil lamp and the woman whose role it is to tend it. In talking about his work, Mattiusi has explained (Spirit Wrestler Gallery 2002): "When you look at my sculpture, you don't understand all of it. For this reason, you have the freedom to dream. Everyone has opinions about art so I just put titles for each piece and leave the rest for dreams." A sculptor for decades, Mattiusi always seems to find something new to say or a new way to approach the sculptural form.

Luke Anowtalik has worked on caribou antler carving since at least the 1970s. As his carvings have become increasingly larger and more complex, each work retains a freshness of its own.

Elizabeth Anghnaqquaq's wall hanging is characteristic of her sewing style that dates back to the late 1960s, but the richness of colour and embroidery stitching makes each of these wall hangings a unique visual delight.

Other artists, like Manasie Akpaliapik, have made a good number of sculptures that experiment with new forms and investigate new subjects, even as they document Inuit life. As he states (Lalonde 2005 [label copy]): "Everything that I'm doing is trying to capture some of the culture...I feel that the only way we can preserve the culture is if people can see it." Manasie's carving in this exhibition shows the sea goddess Sedna with walrus heads where hands would normally be, depicting the episode in the story where her fingers are cut off joint by joint; upon hitting the water, they transform into walruses, seals and whales. His representation of the sea goddess and the two walrus heads is an elegant, flowing form, in stark contrast to his other work, the untitled 1991 sculpture showing an anguished human head with a carved stone liquor bottle sprouting from the top (Lalonde 2005; *Inuit Art Quarterly* 1993).

Then there is Nick Sikkuark, whose imagination seems to know no bounds. Along with Sikkuark's drawings, his sculptures are a mix of different materials and often show rather wild, strange-looking men, worms or objects like flying shamans' heads.

In this exhibition, Toonoo Sharky, departs from his more lyrical style of stone carving to use a variety of different media to fashion the outrageous *Drum Dancers* sculpture.

Michael Massie, from Labrador, has used his training as a silversmith to experiment with, and elaborate on, the lowly teapot. Silver and other materials are fashioned into fancy teapots, bird-like teapots, drum-dancer teapots, surfer teapots or walrus shaped teapots; sometimes the creamer and sugar bowl are included to make the scene more complex. But Michael is also a consummate carver working with stone and other materials. The work included here, *Come Sit and Have Some Tea*, is made of anhydrite, sterling silver, ebony and bone. It provides a wonderful example of what happens when he combines his teapots with stone carving. This work and the others in his recent exhibition at the Spirit Wrestler Gallery in Vancouver were all accompanied by catchy titles and engaging artist's commentaries. Here is what he had to say about *Come Sit and Have Some Tea* (Spirit Wrestler Gallery 2005):

> Originally, I wanted to make a piece of a woman holding a teapot—but, after some reflection, I thought it would be more appropriate to make an image of me with a teapot in my hand ... I figured that as I am the one that makes them, it should be me holding one!
>
> I wanted the figure to be seated, expressing comfort and relaxation—things we associate with the act of taking tea—and the lifted eyebrows, as if to say "Oooh," I am told, are things that I do. There are certain occasions where people take out their best silverware for company, and I wanted this teapot to be along those lines for this piece. I went back to much earlier designs for the form of the teapot, using the irregular planes as in "tea with Pablo" and "little jimmy", and I used the textured surface rather than a polished surface because I wanted you to see the piece for its form, rather than for how it takes in its surroundings. The pot does refer to the bird teapots through the handle on the lid—and I came up with the rope motif for the handle as it is literally connecting the two pieces together.
>
> I am wearing a parka in this work because I have noticed that every time I have tea outdoors, it always tastes better—and it brings back memories of times up north when I have had students in for tea—and they always wore their coats, no matter how long they stayed!

Such a lengthy explanation by the artist is a new component in Inuit art. Artists are now speaking up to title their works, explain them and discuss how they were made, providing information that in the past was often not available. In this exhibition we see Inuit artworks made in conventional form and content that simply present a slice of Inuit life, albeit a visually pleasing one. Alongside them are works that investigate new media, new subjects and unconventional techniques and make reference to events in the world beyond the Arctic. And there are those that reveal more of the personal side of the maker—thoughts, feelings, personal experience—and establish a dialogue between artist and viewer.

Conclusion

Presented here is a selection of work of Inuit artists from Canada and Sámi artists from Norway, Sweden and Finland made between 2000 and 2005. Both cultures have long histories of making specially crafted objects for functional and religious use; the contemporary manifestations of these traditions show varying degrees of connection with previous times as well as clear indications of change. Artworks from both cultures are displayed side by side in this exhibition and their juxtaposition invites comparison in such characteristics as continuing connection to the original culture, size, media, content and reference to the past.

It is not always easy at such a geographical distance from these cultures to know just what is happening right now—it takes time for information about the art to trickle down. The poetic phrase *In the Shadow of the Midnight Sun* emphasizes the distance that separates the Inuit and Sámi from the more populated areas south of them. They are far enough away, in their land of the midnight sun, to retain an element of romantic exoticness for many people. With this exhibition of contemporary Sámi and Inuit art, we experience, through their collective creative expression, their cultural past and current lives.

*Reindeer and caribou both belong to the genus Rangifer; caribou, larger in size, are found in North America; reindeer inhabit Fenno-Scandinavia and may be domesticated. Reindeer from Norway were imported into both Canada and Alaska in the early 20th century and may still be referred to as reindeer. Napachie Pootoogook explained that the caribou on Baffin Island are the smallest in Nunavut because they interbred with the imported reindeer (Blodgett, 1999, 53). In common parlance caribou have antlers and reindeer have horns.

Jean Blodgett

Samene er et urfolk som har bodd på Nordkalotten, i Norge, Sverige, Finland og Russland, også kalt Sápmi, i uminnelige tider. Som den kjente kunstneren Johan Turi skrev i sin bok "Muittalus Samid birra. En bok om samenes liv", fra 1917: "Man har inte hört, at lapparna skulle ha kommit hit någonstädes ifrån".

Samene har levd av det naturen har hatt å by på som fangst, fiske og reindrift, i tillegg til byttehandel med nabofolk og omreisende.

I reindriftsnæringen har folk levd som nomader, og det var ikke praktisk mulig å frakte med seg ting som ikke var nødvendig for å overleve. Bilder og skulpturer kom derfor i siste rekke. Men samene har likevel omgitt seg med kunst i det meste av hverdagen. Rundt omkring i landskapet var det helleristninger og hellige skulpturer, såkalte sieidier, og nesten alt man brukte av gjenstander var dekorert og ornamentert. I tillegg til dette var runebommen med sine mystiske tegn og symboler en viktig del av livet. Samisk håndverk; *duodji*, har overlevd gjennom århundrene, og har ved siden av å være en del av hverdagen til det samiske folket også utviklet seg til en egen kunstart.

Selveste billedkunsten er ganske ny i det samiske samfunnet. Den hadde sin spede begynnelse ved århundreskiftet til nittenhundretallet, med de selvlærte kunstnerne Johan Turi og Nils Nilsson Skum. John Savio var den første samen som tok kunstutdanning. Han hadde sin mest produktive periode på 1920-30- tallet. Deretter fulgte det en hel generasjon før Iver Jåks fra Karasjok startet som duojár, kunsthåndverker, og siden videreutdannet seg til billedkunstner. Fra 1970-tallet har kunstlivet blomstret i Sápmi.

De tidligste kunstverkene

Helleristninger

Helleristninger er bilder eller mønster som er hugd, risset eller slipt inn i bergflater eller på stein. De eldste helleristningene i Nord Skandinavia kan dateres fra ca. 6000 til 4000 år før vår tidsregning. Helleristningene kunne variere noe i utforming. Ofte var de naturalistiske fremstillinger, og naive i sin utforming.

Helleristningene hadde forskjellige motiv, som dyr, fugler og fisk og båter, ski og forskjellige fangstredskaper. Menneskefiguren selv var kanskje den viktigste av alle figurene. Det var forskjellige gjøremål som var beskrevet, som jakt, fiske, dans, befruktning og religiøse handlinger.

Noen motiv er relativt lett å forstå, mens andre har et mer usikkert innhold, kanskje med symbolske betydinger og religiøse forestillinger.

Uavhengig av hvordan helleristningene i Norden er blitt til og hva de har vært brukt til, så har de eksistert i tusenvis av år, og vært med på å sette sitt preg på landskap der mennesker har bodd.

I dag står helleristningene som et minne fra fortiden. Via forskning har ristningene gitt kunnskaper om hvordan folk i området har levd. Samtidig har helleristningene et mystisk preg. De bærer på hemmeligheter som man vanskelig kan finne svar på i vår moderne verden. Kunstnere har opp gjennom tidene latt seg inspirere av disse urgamle bildene og mønstrene som ble risset inn i berg og steiner for tusenvis av år siden.

Den hellige trommen, runebommen

De hellige trommene eller runebommene var vanlig frem til 1700-tallet. De ble brukt til flere forskjellige formål, som for eksempel å se inn i fremtiden. Enkelte som var flinke å bruke trommen kunne joike og tromme seg inn i en slags transe, der de reiste inn i åndenes rike.

Trommene varierte litt i størrelse og utforming. Felles for dem var at de hadde et skinn spent over en tromme-ramme, og de var som oftest oval i formen. Det var vanlig å henge små gjenstander på trommene, for at de skulle få mer kraft. Sterke anheng kunne for eksempel være klør, tenner, metallbiter, eller penis- bein fra bjørn.

Trommene var helt personlige eiendeler, som ble formet av sine eiere. Det var vanlig at trommen gikk i arv og den kunne den følge flere generasjoners liv. Jo eldre den var desto mektigere og mere kraftfylt ble den. På trommeskinnet ble det malt dekorasjoner med en blanding av olderbark og spytt, noe som gjorde fargen blodrød, og den var holdbar i hundrevis av år. Dekorasjonene med figurer, hellige tegn og symboler var hentet fra samisk mytologi og hverdagsliv. Komposisjonen hadde sammenheng med en magisk funksjon. Det var vanlig å illustrere solen, og guder som styrte været var viktige. Ellers var både det onde og det gode representert. Figurer og symboler kunne ofte være lik figurer fra helleristninger, så her kan man kanskje spore en påvirkning.

De fleste trommene ble brent av kristne misjonærer som verken hadde forståelse- eller respekt for samenes kultur. Dermed er et stort materiale forsvunnet. I dag er det svært få ekte trommer tilbake.

Sieidier

I tillegg til trommene hadde samene hellige skulpturer, sieidier, som ble tilbedt og ofret til. Det var helst gjenstander som ble funnet i naturen som så litt merkelig ut, for eksempel en stein som lignet på et ansikt. Fjell, vann og beiteområder kunne også være hellige.

Rundt sieidiene kunne man finne reinhorn og andre gjenstander som samene ofret for å kommunisere med- og blidgjøre åndene. På offerplassene skulle folk være stille, og ikke oppføre seg støyende.

Ifølge samenes gamle tro skulle man ikke fjerne noe fra en offerplass, men la det ligge til naturen hadde fortært det. Horn, bein og tre tar kort tid å forvitre. En mannsalder er ikke lang tid. Kom man til en offerplass skulle man legge igjen noe som et tegn på respekt for gudene.

Under den dansk-norske misjoneringen og kristningen av samene var det vanlig at de ødela sieidiene. Steiner ble veltet og trefigurer brent. Det ble ansett som straffbart å utøve den gamle religionen, noe som kunne få alvorlige konsekvenser for de som brøt forbudet. Til tross for dette klarte enkelte å beholde noen av de gamle skikkene, og dermed sørge for at man i dag har kunnskaper om dette.

Den dag i dag har mange samer stor respekt for de gamle sieidiene, og regner disse fortsatt som hellige.

Samisk kunsthåndverk, duodji

Duodji er betegnelsen for samisk kunsthåndverk, som foruten å ha lange røtter i samisk tradisjon ennå er en svært viktig del av den samiske kulturen. Ordet duodji finnes i alle samiske dialekter og betyr, fritt oversatt; håndverk, håndarbeid og annet arbeid utført for hånd.

Duodji er et samlebegrep som omfatter mange ulike virksomheter fra husflid og håndverk til kunsthåndverk og kunst. Det vil med andre ord si produksjon av alt utstyr som har vært nødvendig for å overleve og for trivsel.

Foruten det estetiske aspektet, som hele tiden har vært viktig, har duodji også vært en nødvendighet. Håndverkets funksjon har vært det viktigste.

En gjenstand ble ikke laget kun for å være til pynt, men for at den skulle kunne brukes til noe nyttig. Formen ble bestemt av hva tingen skulle brukes til. Kunnskaper har gått i arv og har flere hundre års gamle både uavbrutte og bearbeidede tradisjoner i den samiske kulturen. Bruksgjenstander laget av tidligere generasjoner har overlevd fordi de gjennom lang tids bruk har vist seg hensiktsmessige.

Fra gammelt av hadde ikke reindriftssamene anledning til å eie ting som ikke var absolutt nødvendig for å overleve. Eiendelene skulle alltid være tilpasset den nomadiske livsstilen. Krav ble stilt om at tingene skulle være lett å pakke, ikke ha skarpe kanter som kunne ripe opp andre ting, men være butt og avrundet, og de skulle være praktiske. Derfor går ofte de runde formene igjen i det samiske formspråket.

Som skapende virksomhet har duodji en spesiell verdi fordi den styrker samisk stilsans og kulturfølelse og gjør de som utøver virksomheten praktisk delaktig i videreføringen av samiske tradisjoner inn i det moderne samfunnet. Mange samiske kunstnere og kunsthåndverkere arbeider for å utvikle og utvide begrepet duodji, for at den samiske kunsten også skal følge med i nåtiden.

Duodji styrker samisk stilsans og kulturfølelse og fungerer som en bro mellom forfedrenes liv og tradisjoner og nåtidens samfunn. Broen blir bygget med de samme materialene som fortidens samer benyttet; skinn, horn, tre og røtter, en bro bygget med nedarvet sans for form og linjespill.

Tidlige samiske kunstnere

I uminnelige tider har samene behersket kunsten å risse i reinhorn, bein og tre med kniv, for å dekorere gjenstander. Allmenn skolegang gjorde slik at papir og blyanter ble lettere tilgjengelig, noe som igjen førte til at enkelte samer begynte å tegne og lage billedkunst.

Johan Olafsson Turi

Johan Olafsson Turi (1854 – 1936) ble kjent etter at han sammen med den danske kunstnerinnen Emilie Demant forfattet boka "Muittalus Samid birra. En bok om lapparnes liv", som kom ut i 1917. Den tar for seg mange sider ved den samiske kulturen. Boken som er blitt en klassiker, og trykket opp i flere opplag og oversatt til flere språk, er rikt dekorert med tegninger fra forskjellige samiske aktiviteter, gjenstander og forklaringer.

Som kunstner var Turi autodidakt og han hadde et enkelt, naivt formspråk, som minnet om helleristninger. Han behersket ikke perspektivtegning. Motiver var hentet fra reindriftsamenes hverdag, der livet på vidda sto sentralt. Rein var hovedmotiv i bildene, og jo flere rein som var med i bildene desto høyere pris tok han. Når bildene hans begynte å bli populære fant han på å skjære motivene ut som stempel, for at de skulle kunne brukes flere ganger og lette arbeidet.

Nils Nilsson Skum

En annen samisk kunstner som gjorde seg bemerket tidlig på 1900-tallet var Nils Nilsson Skum, (1872-1951). Som Turi var også Skum autodidakt, og hans første tegninger var også perspektivløse. Han arbeidet mye med bildene sine, og hadde fotografisk hukommelse på steder han hadde vært vant å ferdes. Til slutt ble Skum den første samen som brakte naturen inn i billedkunsten, og for å klare dette måtte han bruke perspektivtegning. Teknikken kom intuitivt, men enda klarte han å lage bilder med nesten tredimensjonal virkning. I den senere tid er det blitt klart at også Skum lagde stempel for å rasjonalisere arbeidet. Hans bilder beskrev som Turis` den ytre virkelighet og livet som reindriftssame.

John Andreas Savio

Den mest kjente av de tidlige samiske kunstnerne var John Andreas Savio. Han ble født 1902, i Sør- Varanger i Norge, og han var den første samen som tok utdannelse innen billedkunst. Han behersket både tegning, akvarell og oljemaleri. Mest kjent er han for sine tresnitt. Tresnittene var oftest sort trykk på hvitt papir, men det forekommer også fargetrykk.

Savio kjente sine motiver godt, og var svært treffsikker når han fremstilte både barn, voksne og dyr- i arbeid og lek. Samspillet mellom dyra, naturen og menneskene var vanlige motiver i Savios kunst. Det var sitt eget miljø han skildret. Han gav et bilde på hvordan det føltes å leve og være same. For en som er kjent med Finnmarks lunefulle, og stadig skiftende vær, vil det ikke være vanskelig å kjenne seg igjen i Savios motiver. Han var en mester i å skildre det spesielle lyset i nord og stemningen det fører med seg. Savio laget ikke bare motiver fra den samiske hverdagen. Han har i den senere tid også blitt kjent for andre motiver.

John Andreas Savio ble ikke rik på kunsten sin. Allerede som 36-åring døde han av sykdom i Norges hovedstad, Oslo.

Savio regnes som den mest kjente samiske billedkunstneren, og blir stadig trukket inn i kunstdiskusjoner nesten 70 år etter sin død. I Kirkenes i Sør-Varanger har han fått sitt eget museum, Saviomuseet.

Samisk kunstliv i dag

Det skulle altså gå en hel generasjon før det på nytt dukket opp nye dyktige samiske billedkunstnere etter John Andreas Savio.

Iver Jåks fra Karasjok tok sin utdannelse på 1950-tallet. Han var tidlig ute med å etablere et moderne samisk formspråk, hvor former og symboler har klare forbindelser til den samiske kulturen. Det har også vært viktig for han å følge en samisk håndverkstradisjon, og bruke nedarvede kunnskaper om materialer og tradisjoner i sine arbeider, samtidig som han regnes som en universell kunstner.

For inntil få år siden var Iver Jåks en aktiv billedkunstner og debattant, og han har markert seg som kunstner både i Norge og utlandet. Hans kunstverk og teorier har inspirert mange kunstnere etter han, og han er vår største, nålevende, samiske kunstner.

Andre kunstnere kom raskt etter, og på 1970- tallet var det flere unge samer som utdannet seg på kunstakademi og høgskoler.

Samisk kunstnergruppe var en idealistisk gjeng med nyutdannede kunstnere som sammen flyttet til den samiske bygden Masi for å arbeide som kunstnere. De ble derfor også kalt Masigruppen. Som kunstnere hadde de forskjellige uttrykk og utgangspunkt. Materialbruk og motivvalg var inspirert både av vestlige strømninger og av egen kultur og opphav. Felles for dem var at de var svært bevisste på sin samiske identitet, og de arbeidet aktivt for å fremme den samiske kulturen.

Dette skjedde samtidig med en kulturell oppvåkning i det samiske folket, som hadde vært undertrykt av majoritetssamfunnet. Selv i flere tiår etter 2. verdenskrig ble det samiske folket utsatt for en massiv fornorskning, som gjør at språket, den sterkeste markøren for samisk identitet, i dag bare snakkes av noen få tusen.

For å redde samekulturen spilte de samiske billedkunstnerne en svært viktig rolle. De var politisk bevisste og fikk mange til å bli stolt av sitt opphav i stedet for å forsøke å skjule det.

Samiske Kunstneres Forbund

I 1979 ble organisasjonen Samiske Kunstneres Forbund dannet som et resultat av arbeidet Samisk Kunstnergruppe i Masi hadde gjort, i tillegg til behovet den stadig økende gruppen av samiske kunstnere hadde for et samlende forum på tvers av landegrensene i Sápmi. Samiske Kunstneres Forbund er i dag en livskraftig, faglig organisasjon som har til oppgave å ivareta og fremme samiske kunstneres interesser. De arbeider aktivt for å synliggjøre samiske kunstnere og deres arbeider.

Rundt regnet 70 billedkunstnere og kunsthåndverkere er medlem av Samisk Kunstnerforbund i dag. Medlemmene kommer fra alle de fire landene i Sápmi, men Russland er foreløpig bare representert med et medlem.

Samisk Kunstmuseum

En annen institusjon som er viktig for samisk kunst er Sámiid Vuorká-Dávvirat/ De Samiske Samlinger i Karasjok. Her ligger kunstavdelingen som gjennom årtier har vært mottagerinstitusjon for offentlige innkjøp av samisk billedkunst.

Sametinget i Norge bevilger n.kr. 350 000, - i året for innkjøp av billedkunst og duodji, i tillegg til at Sámiid Vuorká-Dávvirat/ De Samiske Samlinger er mottagerinstitusjon for innkjøp fra Norsk Kulturråd. Samlingen består i dag av ca. 760 kunstverk. Innkjøpene er gjort systematisk over flere tiår, og samlingen representerer dermed en unik kontinuitet i det beste innen samisk kunst. Det viktigste arbeidet for Sámiid Vuorká-Dávvirat/ De Samiske Samlingers kunstavdeling i dag er å få en bygning hvor disse kunstverkene kan vises samlet, et samisk kunstmuseum, og dermed bli en enda viktigere aktør i arbeidet for å fremme den samiske kulturen. Kunstnerne på denne utstillingen

Kunstnerne på denne utstillingen

På denne utstillingen får publikum et lite inntrykk av mangfoldet innen den samiske kunstverden, og hva et fremtidig Samisk Kunstmuseum vil kunne by på.

Vi kan se **Iria Čiekča Schmidt** Jaktgudinne, som viser tilbake til gammel samisk religion og gudstro, hvor de mektige gudinnene hadde en sentral plass i menneskenes liv, og hjalp til i hverdagen og i kritiske faser i menneskers og dyrs liv.

Per Enokssons bilder skaper forundring med sitt tvetydige innhold. Hans arbeider har en intens energi, som utfordrer tilskueren med sin fortellerglede.

Bente Gevings nære og sterkt poetiske bilder får kjente motiver til å fremstå som noe annet. Ved at de er satt sammen to og to, åpner de hverandre til en ny poetisk stemning. Vi inviteres inn i et annet univers.

Marja Helander er samejenta som er vokst opp i Helsinki, Finlands hovedstad. I hennes fotoprosjekt "Nomad" gjennomfører hun et slags etnisk rollespill i jakten på egen identitet. Fotografiene er både alvorlige og ironiske, som for eksempel der hun har på seg en lysgrå drakt og sko med høye heler, men hun er samtidig plassert helt feil, i et snødekt landskap på vidda. Hun hører til to folk, og det er forventet at hun skal justere sin identitet etter ulike sammenhenger.

Arnold Johansens bilde av naturlandskapet "Kråkungan" er et fotoprint som er brettet i en teknikk som gjør at motivet forandrer seg ettersom hvor betrakteren står. Ved å bevege seg fra den ene siden til den andre kan man se skiftningene i lyset i et fantastisk, arktisk vinterlandskap.

Det store portrettet "Mats" er laget i en spesiell teknikk, og fremstår som nesten utydelig og flimerede i formen. Utgangspunktet er et ordinært fotografi som er blitt scannet inn, og deretter kjørt gjennom en spesiell digital filtreringsprosess som gir motivet dette spesielle preget av stripete rastrer.

Hilde Skancke Pedersens arbeider "Livstegn" tar på en varsom måte opp i seg fargene i det samiske flagget, rødt, grønt, blått og gult. Små spirer forsøker å trenge gjennom det kalde, harde snødekket og bli til liv. Dette kan være en illustrasjon på det harde livet på vidda, men også håp og mot.

Monica L. Edmondsons nyskapende og flotte glasskunst spiller også på fargene fra det samiske flagget, og samisk klesdrakt. Dette har hun bundet sammen med en teknikk som kalles murrini som er en gammel italiensk teknikk romerne hentet fra Egypt i tiden rundt Kristi fødsel.

Hege Annestad Nilsen har tatt portrettbilder av sin familie, hvor de er plassert i sitt hjemlige miljø. I hendene holder de opp bilder av seg selv som barn. Med dette bygger hun en bro mellom fortid og nåtid, hvor identitet er et viktig tema. Hvem er jeg og hvem var jeg? Har tiden som har gått forandret min identitet?

Inga Nordsletta Pedersens vev heter "Gollegiisa", som på norsk betyr gullskrinet. Samer i både nye og gamle drakter sitter rundt et skrin, og en nøkkel henger oppe på veven. Det samiske språket kalles ofte for gollegiella, gullspråket. Dette kan være en metafor på den samiske kulturen. Hvor de som har nøkkelen til skrinet, samekulturen, har en godt bevart skatt.

Outi Pieski er den yngste kunstneren som deltar på denne utstillingen fra samisk side. Pieski har en fri og eksperimentell teknikk, hvor hun maler på tøy og klistrer sukkertøypapir, som blinker og glinser. Resultatet blir en eventyraktig skog, fylt av mystikk og omkranset av de merkelige lysfenomener man finner inne på vidda i landet mot nord.

Alf Salo maler innenfor en abstrakt konstruktivistisk tradisjon. Formspråket underbygges av fargevalget som er holdt i røde og oransje nyanser. Forholdet mellom farge og form gjør at bildene gir inntrykk av å være i bevegelse. En stram komposisjon holder bildet samlet, mens rette linjer spiller mot myke former. En knivskarp linjeføring med rekker av mønsterbånd gir assosiasjoner til duodji og samisk ornamenttradisjon.

Annelise Josefsen er billedhugger og meisler ut sine skulpturer av store granittblokker. Motivene finnes allerede inne i steinen, og hun hjelper de å komme ut. Lilledama, som vises på denne utstillingen har et erotisk preg, der kvinnefiguren rolig sitter og lener seg mot en stor fallos. Erotikken er en naturlig del av mennesket, og går ofte igjen i samisk kunst. Josefsens steinskulpturer minner om de gamle sieidiene, der falloslignende figurer hadde stor kraft.

Johanne Losoa Larssons store maleri "Blå natur" viser et lett abstrahert landskap. De vakre blåtonene i bildet gir assosiasjoner til intense naturopplevelser.

Synnøve Persen er i likhet med Britta Marakatt-Labba og Josef Halse en av kunstnerne fra den tidligere omtalte Masigruppen. Hun arbeider med abstrakt maleri, der man treffer på kontraster mellom harde mørke flater, som antyder en indre konflikter, og myke former som balanseres av duse farger, ofte med en søken innover i maleriets muligheter.

Josef Halses fargebruk bringer oss brytningene i naturen, i overganger fra vinter til vår, kombinert med rytmer fra naturen, med gjentagelser, kontraster og luft. Det er energi og bevegelse i hans arbeider, en maktkamp mellom intellektet og det spontane.

Britta Marakatt-Labba broderer sine bilder med ørsmå sting, og kombinerer på denne måten gammelt håndverk med ny billedtradisjon. Motivene henter hun fra erfaringer fra egen kulturbakgrunn, i sagn og hendelser som har preget hennes liv.

Ingunn Utsis skulptur "Den med gittervindu og drømmer om frihet" er et spennende arbeid. Skulpturen er laget av den flere hundre år gamle tresorten Passvikfuru, fra Norges nordøstligste sted. I tillegg til furu har hun dekorert skulpturen med glass, fjær, rav og stein, som gjør at betrakteren kan gå på en slags skattejakt, og stadig finne nye detaljer. Skulpturen har et elegant drag over seg, der treet nesten slynger seg opp i luften. Det kan ligne både fuglevinger eller en hvalspord. Skulpturen er malt solgul på yttersiden, mens den er mørk brun inni. Kvister og hull er aksentuert med mørkere farger eller fylt med fjær. Assosiasjonene går til fugleøynene, som her er blitt helt abstrahert. Spenningen er også knyttet til en dualitet mellom det innestengte og det frie, det lyse og det mørke. Det handler om frihetsberøvelse og drømmen om et annet sted, eller en annen tilstand. Romlige former som også skaper stengsler. En skjønnhet som ikke bare er god, men også problematisk.

Med på denne utstillingen er også 4 duodjiarbeider i høy kvalitet.

Sune Enoksson har laget en guksi, som er et tradisjonelt øse- og drikkeredskap. Kunstneren har kombinert materialene tre, elghorn og sølv. Skaftet og undersiden på guksien er ornamentert med strenge geometriske mønster, noe som er vanlig i sydsamiske områder.

Per Isak Juuso har laget en runebomme etter gammel tradisjon. Figurene på trommeskinnet er plassert på horisontale linjer, noe som var vanlig på nordsamiske trommer. På trommens bakside har han risset inn et akantuslignende mønster, og runebommehammeren har også et lignede mønster. En friere ornamentikk, uten de strenge geometriske linjene er også noe man finner i de nordsamisk områdene.

Nils Arvid Westerfjell har laget en utsøkt beltering, med alle redskapene kvinnen trengte å bære på seg i hverdagen, som kniv, skje, nålehus og saks. Ringer i messing er festet på redskapene, noe man i tidligere tider gjorde for å beskytte seg mot onde krefter.

Max Lundström har kombinert gammel materialkunnskap med et nyere formspråk, og ut av dette har han formet en eksklusiv bolle. Samtlige av disse kunsthåndverkerne er med på å bringe kunnskap fra tidligere generasjoner frem til neste.

Hva er samisk samtidskunst?

Samiske kunstnere er en svært sammensatt gruppe. Den eneste klare fellesnevneren man ser i dag er egentlig at kunstnerne er samer. De har det til felles at de har tilknytning til to folk, til majoritetssamfunnet på den ene siden, og det samiske på den andre. Selv om man kan spore enkelte fellestrekk i valg av motiver og materialbruk med opphav i egen kulturbakgrunn hos enkelte, vil en generalisering ut over dette være feil.

Den tidlige samiske billedkunsten hadde en tendens til å understreke og illustrere samiskhet, mens man i dag ser et mer komplisert og sammensatt bilde. Selv om man kan spore elementer av etnisk tilknytning i mange kunstverk, trenger ikke et uøvet øye å se dette. Elementer fra egen kulturbakgrunn er mer skjult, og noen kunstnere føler det nesten som beklemmende å hele tiden møte en forventing om at deres arbeider skal handle om det samiske. Det er også tydelig at flere kunstnere ikke bare orienterer seg mot en europeisk eller vestlig billedtradisjon, men beveger seg ut over dette og er i dialog med en global verden.

Samisk samtidskunst sier noe om dagen i dag. Om hvordan det føles å være same.
Kunsten sier noe om hva som er viktig i deres liv, slik den også gjorde for de første samiske kunstnere.

Irene Snarby

SÁMI ART

The Sámi are an indigenous people who have lived on the *Nordkalotten* (North Calotte area) in Norway, Sweden, Finland, and Russia, also known as *Sápmi*, from time immemorial. As the famous artist Johan Turi wrote in his 1917 book, *Muittalus Sámid birra*, a book on the life of the Sámi: "We have never heard it said that the Sámi came from anywhere else."

The Sámi have always lived from what nature has to offer, hunting, fishing and reindeer herding, as well as trading with neighbors and itinerants.

Reindeer herding is a nomadic lifestyle, and it was just not practical to cart around anything not critical for survival. Paintings and sculptures were therefore the lowest priority. But the Sámi still surrounded themselves with art in their everyday life. All around the landscape were rock carvings and sacred sculptures, so-called "*sieidier*," and nearly every object used was decorated and ornamented. Additionally, the *runebomme*, or sacred drum, with its mystical signs and symbols, was an important part of life. Sámi handicrafts – *duodji* – have survived for centuries, and have, in addition to being an integral part of everyday life for the Sámi people, also developed into a separate art category.

Even painting is relatively new in Sámi society. It had its tender infancy at the turn of the last century, with self-taught artists Johan Turi and Nils Nilsson Skum. John Savio was the first Sámi to take art training. His most productive period was in the 1920s and 30s. A whole generation passed before Iver Jåks from Karasjok began as *duojár*, craftsman, and eventually received further training as an artist. Since the 1970s, art has bloomed in Sápmi.

The earliest works of art

Rock carvings

Rock carvings are pictures or patterns sculpted, sketched, or ground into mountainsides or onto stone. The oldest rock carvings in Northern Scandinavia date from around 6,000 to 4,000 years B.C.E. Rock carvings could vary somewhat in their design. They were often naturalistic depictions, and naïve in their design.

Rock carvings had different subjects such as animals, birds, fish, boats, skis, and different hunting tools. The human figure itself was perhaps the most important of all figures. Different tasks were depicted, such as hunting, fishing, dancing, fertilization, and religious ceremonies.

Some of the subjects are relatively easy to understand, while others - perhaps with symbolical significance and religious depictions - are less clear.

No matter how rock carvings in the North came to be and what they were used for, they have existed for thousands of years, and have made their mark on the landscape where humans have lived.

Today rock carvings stand as a memory from the past. Through research, the carvings have taught us how people in the area lived. They also have a mystical influence. They hold secrets that are difficult to understand in our modern world. Through the ages, artists have found inspiration in these age-old pictures and patterns chiseled into mountain and stone thousands of years ago.

The sacred drum, *runebommen*

The sacred drum, or *runebommen*, was commonplace up until the 1700s. These drums were put to various uses, for example, to look into the future. Certain elders could chant and drum themselves into a kind of trance, during which they voyaged to the realm of the spirit.

The drums varied somewhat in size and design. All consisted of an animal skin stretched over a drum frame, and they were usually oval in shape. It was common to hang small objects on the drums, to make them more powerful. Some examples of these objects are talons, teeth, pieces of metal, or penis bones from a bear.

The drums were extremely personal belongings, designed by their owners and passed down through the generations. The older the drum, the more powerful it became. The drum skins were decorated with paint made from a mixture of elder bark and spit, which resulted in a blood red colour that lasted hundreds of years. Decorations with figures, holy signs, and symbols were taken from Sámi mythology and everyday life. The composition was linked to a magic function. It was common to depict the sun, and the gods that controlled the weather were important. Both good and bad were depicted. Figures and symbols could often resemble figures from rock carvings, so here perhaps we detect an influence.

Christian missionaries, who neither understood, nor respected, the Sámi culture, burned most drums, leaving very few in existence today.

Sacred sculptures

As well as the drums, the Sámi had sacred sculptures – *sieidier* – to which supplications and sacrifices were made. Usually, these were rather unusual-looking objects found in nature, for example a stone that resembled a face. Mountains, water, and grazing grounds could also be considered sacred.

Around the stone sculptures could be found reindeer antlers and other objects the Sámi sacrificed in order to communicate with and appease the spirits. At these sacrificial sites, people had to be quiet, and not behave in a noisy fashion.

In accordance with the ancient Sámi belief, nothing was to be removed from a sacrificial site, but should remain until consumed by nature. Antlers, bones, and wood disintegrated within a very short time. If one came across a sacrificial site, one would leave something behind as a sign of respect for the gods.

When Danish-Norwegian missionaries brought Christianity to the Sámi, it was common to destroy sacred sculptures. The stones were toppled and the wooden figures burned. Practicing the old religion was banned, and those who ignored this order were severely punished. In spite of this, a few Sámi managed to uphold some of the old customs, thereby making it possible for us to have this knowledge today.

Today, many Sámi have great respect for the old *sieidies*, and still regard them as sacred.

Sámi crafts (*duodji*)

Duodji is the term used for Sámi handicrafts, which as well as being deeply rooted in Sámi tradition, still play a major role in Sámi culture. The word *duodji* can be found in all Sámi dialects, and means, loosely translated; crafts, needlework, and other work carried out by hand.

Duodji is a compound concept that includes many different industries, from homemade articles and crafts to art wares and art, i.e., production of all equipment needed for survival and for well-being.

In addition to the esthetic aspect, which has always been important, *duodji* has also been a necessity. The item's functionality has always been key.

Objects were never made merely to serve as decoration, but to be put to some use. The design was determined by the object's usage. This knowledge was passed down from generation to generation, and has several centuries of both unbroken and adapted traditions in Sámi culture. Fine objects created by earlier generations have survived precisely because they have proved useful.

Since the olden days, Sámi who raised reindeer owned only that which was necessary for survival. Possessions had to be adapted to the nomadic lifestyle. Thus, objects had to be easy to pack, blunt and rounded to avoid damaging other things, and practical. This explains why we so often observe the rounded form in Sámi design.

As a creative industry, the *duodji* is of particular value since it strengthens the Sámi sense of style and cultural sensitivity, and involves those who perform the activity on a practical level in the further development of Sámi traditions in today's society. Many Sámi artists and crafts people work to develop and broaden the *duodji* concept, to ensure that Sámi art keeps up with the present.

Duodji strengthens the Sámi sense of style and cultural sensitivity, and functions as a bridge between the ancestors' life and traditions, and today's society. This bridge has been built using materials of old skins, as Sámi from earlier days used; skin, antlers, wood and roots a bridge built with an inherited sense of design and the play of lines.

Earlier Sámi artists

From time immemorial, the Sámi have mastered the art of engraving reindeer antlers, bones, and wood with a knife. Universal education made paper and pencils more easily accessible, and resulted in a number of Sámi beginning to draw and to make pictures.

Johan Olafsson Turi

Johan Olafsson Turi (1854-1936) became known after he (along with Danish artist Emilie Demant), authored the book, **Muittalus Sámid birra. En bok om lapparnas liv** (*A book on the life of the Sámi*), which was published in 1917. The book, which describes the many facets of Sámi culture, became a classic, was reprinted several times and translated into several languages. It is richly decorated, and contains drawings depicting different Sámi activities and objects, and explanations.

Turi was a self-taught artist with a simple, naïve language of design, which brings to mind the rock carvings. He did not master perspective drawing. The themes he chose came from the everyday life of Sámi involved in raising reindeer, where life in the wide open spaces was the central focus. Reindeer were the principal theme of his pictures, and the more reindeer in a picture, the more he charged for it. As his pictures became popular, he found making a re-usable stamp of each of his subjects made his work easier.

Nils Nilsson Skum

Another Sámi artist who made a name for himself in the early 1900s was Nils Nilsson Skum (1872-1950). Like Turi, Skum was self-taught, and his first drawings were also lacking in perspective. But he worked hard on his pictures, and had a photographic memory of the places he visited. He was the first Sámi to bring nature into the art of painting, and to manage that, he was obliged to use perspective. Although the technique came to him intuitively, he still managed to make pictures with nearly three-dimensional effect. In later years Skum, too, used stamps to standardize his work. His pictures, like Turi's, depicted the outdoor activities and life of the Sámi reindeer herders.

John Andreas Savio

The best known of the earlier Sámi artists was John Andreas Savio. Born in Sør-Varanger, Norway, in 1902, he was the first Sámi who trained in art. He mastered drawing, watercolours and oils, but was best known for his woodcuttings. These were most often printed black on white paper, but there were also some colour prints.

Savio knew his subjects well, and had a very sure stroke when he depicted children, adults, and animals – at work and at play. The interaction between the animals, nature, and humans, was the usual theme of Savio's art.

He portrayed his own milieu. He showed how it felt to live, and to be, Sámi. Anyone familiar with Finnmark's capricious, constantly changing, weather will easily recognize Savio's subjects. He was a master at catching that special Northern light of the North, and the atmosphere it creates. However, Savio also chose other subjects, and became known for these in later years.

John Andreas Savio never became rich from his art, and died after an illness at the age of 36, in Oslo, Norway.

Savio is considered the most well known Sámi painter, and is still mentioned in discussions of art nearly 70 years after his death. A museum dedicated to his work, Saviomuseet, is located in Kirkenes in Sør-Varangar.

Sámi artistic life today

After John Andreas Savio, a whole generation passed before once again new, talented Sámi artists appeared on the scene.

Iver Jåks from Karasjok took his training in the 1950s. He quickly established a modern Sámi language of design, with designs and symbols that had a connection to Sámi culture. It has also been important for him to follow a Sámi hand work tradition, and he used inherited knowledge about materials and traditions in his works, while still being regarded as a universal artist.

Until a few years ago, Iver Jåks was an active painter and discussant, and he has a reputation as an artist both in Norway and abroad. His art works and theories have inspired many artists following in his steps, and he is our greatest living Sámi artist.

Other artists followed quickly, and in the 1970s several young Sámi were trained at the art academies and high schools.

The Sámi art group was an idealistic gang of freshly trained artists who moved to the Sámi village Masi to work together as artists. They became known as the *Masigruppen*, or Masi Group. As artists they had different ways of expressing themselves, and different starting points. The use of materials and the choice of subjects were inspired both by the West, and by their own culture and origins. What they had in common was that they were certain of their Sámi identity, and they worked actively to promote Sámi culture.

This took place in tandem with a cultural awakening amongst Sámi people, who had previously been oppressed by a society in which they were a minority. Even several decades after WWII, the Sámi people of Norway were subjected to a massive assimilation campaign; today, their language – the strongest symbol of Sámi identity – is spoken by only a few thousand people.

Sámi artists played an important role in safeguarding their culture. They were politically savvy and made many people proud of their origins, instead of trying to hide them.

The Sámi Artists' Union

In 1979, the Sámi Artists' Union was founded as a result of the work by the Sámi artists' group in Masi, and in response to the need of the steadily increasing number of Sámi artists spread across the Sápmi country borders. The Sámi Artists' Union today is a vital, professional association whose mandate is to safeguard and promote the interests of Sámi artists. They strive to give visibility to Sámi artists and their work.

Today, the Sámi Artists' Union numbers about 70 artists among its members. They come from all the Sápmi countries, but Russia currently has only one member.

The Sámi Art Museum

Another institution that is important for Sámi art is *De Sámiske Samlinger* (Sámi Museum) in Karasjok. The art department here has for several decades been the recipient of official purchases of Sámi art.

The Sámi Parliament votes 350,000 Norwegian kroner per annum for the purchase of art, and the Sámi Museum also houses works of art purchased by the Norwegian Cultural Council. The collection today comprises approximately 760 works of art. Since the art works have been purchased systematically over several decades, the collection represents a unique continuity in the best of Sámi art. The most important effort for the Sámi Museum today is to acquire a building where these works of art can be displayed together, a Sámi art museum, and thus become an even more important player in the effort to promote Sámi culture.

Sámi Artists Featured in the Exhibition

This exhibition gives the public a brief impression of the multiplicity within the Sámi world of art, and suggests what a future Sámi Art Museum will offer.

We can see **Iria Čiekča Schmidt's** *Leaibolmmái/Jaktgudinnen* (The Goddess of Hunting), which takes us back to ancient Sámi religion and belief in gods, when the powerful goddess was central to people's lives, providing assistance in both the day-to-day and critical phases of people's and animals' lives.

Per Enoksson's paintings, with their ambiguous content, surprise us. His works have an intense energy that challenges the viewer with its joy of narration.

Bente Geving's intimate and strongly poetic pictures make known subjects appear as something quite different. The way they are placed, side-by-side, opens each of them to a new poetic atmosphere, and we are invited into another universe.

Marja Helander is a Sámi woman who grew up in Helsinki, the capital of Finland. In her photo project, *Nomad/Utsjoki, Finland*, she carries out a kind of ethnic role-playing in the search for her own identity. The photographs are serious and ironic. For example, in one photo she wears a pale gray suit and high-heeled shoes, but is situated quite jarringly in a snow-covered landscape in the plains. She belongs to two peoples, and it is expected that she will adjust her identity to different circumstances.

Arnold Johansen's landscape, *Kraakungan* (Baby Crows), is a photo print that is bent using a technique that results in the subject changing depending on where the viewer stands. By moving from one side to another, we can see – through the changes in light – a fantastic, arctic, winter landscape.

The large picture, *Mats*, was created using a special technique, and emerges as almost indistinct and flickering in its design. The starting point is an ordinary photograph that is scanned, then submitted to a special digital filtering process that gives the subject this special impression of a striped screen.

Hilde Skancke Pedersen's *Livstegn* (Sign of life) gently incorporates the colours of the Sámi flag – red, green, blue, and yellow. Small sprouts attempt to push their way up through the cold, hard, surface of snow, and come to life. This could illustrate the hard life of the wide Northern expanses, but also hope, and courage.

Monica L. Edmondson's creative and beautiful glass art also plays on the colours of the Sámi flag and Sámi attire. She ties these together using a technique called *murrini*, an old Italian technique the Romans brought back from Egypt around the time of Christ's birth.

Hege Annestad Nilsen has taken portraits of her family, all situated in their home environment. In their hands, they hold pictures of themselves as children. Thus, she builds a bridge between the future and the present, where identity is an important theme. Who am I, and who was I? Has the passing of time changed my identity?

Inga Nordsletta Pedersen's woven work is called *Gollegiisa,* which in Norwegian means golden jewellery casket. Sámi in both new and ancient attire sit around a jewellery casket, and a key hangs from the woven fabric. The Sámi language is often called *gollegiella*, or the golden language. This could be a metaphor for Sámi culture, where those who possess the key to the casket – the Sámi culture – have a well-guarded treasure.

Outi Pieski is the youngest artist represented at this exhibition from the Sámi side. Pieski's technique is free and experimental. She paints on cloth and on sticky candy wrappers that sparkle and glisten. The result is a fairytale forest, full of mystique and encircled by the strange light phenomena that can be found in wide open spaces in the northern country.

Alf Salo paints within an abstract, constructivist tradition. The language of design is underpinned by the choice of colour – red and orange nuances. The relationship between colour and form makes the picture appear to be in movement. A taut composition holds the picture together, while straight lines play against soft forms. Knife-sharp lines, featuring rows of patterned bands, provide associations to *duodji* and traditional Sámi ornamentation.

Annelise Josefsen is a sculptor who chisels her sculptures from large blocks of granite. Her subjects are already to be found in the stone; she helps them emerge. *Lilledama* (Little Lady), which is featured in this exhibition, shows an erotic influence. The female figure sits calmly, leaning against a large phallus. Eroticism is a natural element of humanity, and often figures in Sámi art. Josefsen's stone sculptures are reminiscent of the old sacred stone sculptures, where phallic figures held great power.

Johanne Losoa Larsson's large painting, *Blå natur* (Blue Nature), shows a slightly abstract landscape. The beautiful blue tones in the picture provide associations to intense natural experiences.

Synnøve Persen is, along with Britta Marakatt-Labba and Josef Halse, one of the artists belonging to the previously mentioned *Masigruppen*. She works with abstract paintings, which feature contrasts between hard dark surfaces, often representing inner conflicts, and soft shapes balanced by mellow colours, suggesting the subtleties inherent in the painting.

Josef Halse's use of colour brings us nature's refractions, in passages from winter to spring, combined with nature's rhythms, with repetitions, contrasts and air. There is energy and movement in his work, a power struggle between the intellect and the spontaneous.

Britta Marakatt-Labba uses tiny stitches to embroider her pictures, thus combining old crafts with a new picture tradition. She draws her subjects from experiences from her own cultural background, and from legends and events that have influenced her life.

Ingunn Utsi's sculpture, *Den med gittervindu og drømmer om frihet* (The One with a Lattice Window and Dreams of Freedom), is an exciting work. The sculpture is composed of several centuries old *Passvikfuru* wood, from Norway's northernmost area. In addition to the pine, she has also decorated the sculpture with glass, feathers, amber and stone, so that the viewer can follow a sort of treasure hunt, continually discovering new details. The sculpture is elegant, with the wood seeming to fling itself up into the air. It could be said to resemble the wings of a bird, or a whale's tail. The sculpture is painted sunshine yellow on the exterior, but dark brown on the interior. Knots and holes are accentuated with darker colours or filled with feathers. The associations are to birds' eyes, which, here, have become totally abstract. The excitement also comes from a duality between the imprisoned and the free, the light and the dark. It speaks of the loss of liberty and of the dream of a different place, or a different condition. Spacious shapes also create barriers, suggesting a beauty that is not wholly good, but also problematic.

Included in the exhibition are also four high-quality duodji works.

Sune Enoksson has made a *guksi* (Sámi cup), a traditional tool for ladling and drinking. The artist has combined three materials: wood, elk antlers, and silver. The handle and underside of the cup are decorated with the strong geometric patterns common in South Sámi areas.

Per Isak Juuso has crafted a *runebomme* (sacred drum), following ancient tradition. Figures on the drum skin are placed in horizontal lines, as was common with North Sámi drums. On the back of the drum, and on the hammer, he has engraved a pattern that resembles an acanthus leaf. A less controlled ornamentation, without the strong geometric lines, is something one also finds in the North Sámi areas.

Nils Arvid Westerfjell has fashioned an exquisite belt ring with all the tools a woman needed to carry with her in her day-to-day life, such as a knife, spoon, needle case and scissors. Brass rings are attached to the tools, as was done in earlier times to provide protection against evil powers.

Max Lundström has combined ancient knowledge of materials with a newer language of design, and from this has created a unique bowl.

Together, these various and varied forms of craftsmanship bring us knowledge from earlier generations right through to the next.

What is contemporary Sámi art?

Sámi artists are a very complex group. The only clear common denominator to be found today is really that the artists are Sámi. What they have in common is their connection to people, to the majority society on the one side, and to the Sámi on the other. Even though we can spot in some of them certain common characteristics in their choice of subject matter and use of materials, originating in their own cultural background, it would be a mistake to generalize.

The earlier Sámi pictures had a tendency to underline and illustrate "Sámi-ness", while today we see a more complicated and complex picture. Though we can find elements of ethnic correlation in many works of art, it takes a trained eye to see this. Elements from the artist's own cultural background are more hidden, and some artists feel that it is almost suffocating to always have to meet an expectation that the subject of their works will always be the Sámi. It is also plain to see that some artists orient themselves not only towards a European or western tradition, but further, to a dialogue with a global world.

Contemporary Sámi art speaks to the present and explores what it feels like to be Sámi. The art speaks about something important in their lives, just as it did for the first Sámi artists.

Irene Snarby

The Artists and their Works

Manasie Akpaliapik
(b. 1955)
Arctic Bay, Nunavut and Wakefield, Quebec

Sedna and Walruses
2002
Alabaster and whalebone
32 x 61 x 13 cm
On loan from Gallery Phillip, Toronto

In stories about the origins of the sea goddess Sedna there is an episode where her fingers are cut off joint by joint; falling into the water they are transformed into such sea creatures as walruses, seals and whales.

Elizabeth Angrnaqquaq
(1916-2003)
Baker Lake, Nunavut

Animals and People
2000
Wool, felt and embroidery floss
93 x 70 cm
On loan from John and Joyce Price, Seattle

Luke Anowtalik

(b. 1932)

Arviat, Nunavut

Drum Dance

2005

Antler, wood and sinew

40.5 x 84 x 56 cm

Collection of Limperes-Lostaunau Trust

Arnaqu Ashevak

(b. 1956)

Cape Dorset, Nunavut

Evening Landscape

2001

Pencil crayon and ink

50.8 x 66 cm

On loan from John and Joyce Price, Seattle

Arnaqu Ashevak

(b. 1956)

Cape Dorset, Nunavut

Vase with Arctic Grasses

2004

Stone and antler

51.5 x 38 x 35.5 cm

On loan from John and Joyce Price, Seattle

Arnaqu Ashevak

(b. 1956)

Cape Dorset, Nunavut

Memorial

2004

Stone, antler and metal

35 x 23 x 16.5 cm

On loan from Christopher Bredt and

Jamie Cameron, Toronto

"It's symbolic, like a memorial. Up here, sometimes people get lost out on the land and are never found. This is for the people who look for them—the rescue people—and the ones who are lost. I was thinking about those twin towers in New York and how they have a memorial for them. The flower is to remember the people, and the kudlik [oil lamp] is a traditional thing that was very useful for the family up north" (Arnaqu Ashevak in *Kenojuak and Onward*, Feheley Fine Arts 2004).

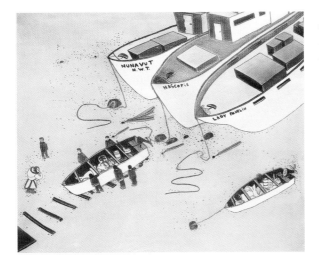

Shuvinai Ashoona

(b. 1961)
Cape Dorset, Nunavut

Low Tide
2003
Etching and aquatint printed by Studio PM,
Montreal
60.6 x 76 cm
On loan from Dorset Fine Arts, Toronto

Shuvinai Ashoona

(b. 1961)
Cape Dorset, Nunavut

Untitled (Church Interior)
2004
Felt tip pen and coloured pencil
66 x 51 cm
Collection of The Winnipeg Art Gallery; acquired
with funds from the Winnipeg Rh Foundation Inc.

Monica L. Edmondson

(b. 1963)
Tärnaby, Sweden

Ellipse II
2005
Hotworked murrini, kilnformed, wheelcut and
etched glass
4 cm x 47-51 cm diameter
On loan from the artist

Monica L. Edmondson

(b. 1963)
Tärnaby, Sweden

Blue Yonder, Close at Heart #11
2005
11 cm x 53.5 cm diameter
Hotworked murrini, kilnformed and wheelcut glass
On loan from Jamie Cameron and
Christopher Bredt, Toronto

Per Enoksson
(b. 1965)
Umeå, Sweden

Sweet Brother, Stupid Sister
2002
Oil and acrylic on canvas
190 x 220 cm
On loan from the County Council of Västerbotten,
Sweden

"The title is about the relation between Norway and Sweden.
Like brother and sister teasing each other about which one is
the best. People in Norway used to call Sweden big brother in
a sarcastic tone. And Sweden doesn't care about Norway and
just says stupid sister"
Per Enoksson, September 2005.

Per Enoksson
(b. 1965)
Umeå, Sweden

Queen Hotel
2002
Oil, acrylic and ink on canvas
180 x 165 cm
On loan from the National Public Art Council,
Sweden

Sune Enoksson
(b. 1934)
Tärnaby, Sweden

Dobbelkosa [Cup]
2000
Wood, reindeer horn and silver
4 x 7 x 11.7 cm
On loan from Sámi Museum,
De Samiske Samlinger, Karasjok, Norway

Isaci Etidloie
(b. 1972)
Cape Dorset, Nunavut

Shaman from the Story of Atanarjuat
2002
Stone, antler and hair
40.5 x 13 x 18 cm
On loan from John and Joyce Price, Seattle

"This is a story I know from the Inuit film Atanarjuat—
we just rented it from the Northern Store in Cape Dorset.
I was thinking of the part when the evil shaman used rabbit's
feet to poison the other fellow. This is the shaman, with his
bones and the design on his parka in hair"
(Isaci Etidloie in *Catching the Eye*, Feheley Fine Arts 2003).

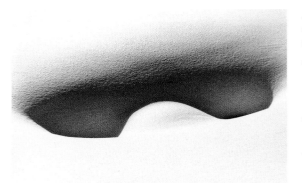

Bente Geving
(b. 1952)
Atrå, Norway

Valfart [Pilgramage] ***8***
2001
Photograph
50 x 75 cm
Nordnorsk Kunstmuseum, Tromsø, Norway

Bente Geving
(b. 1952)
Atrå, Norway

Valfart [Pilgrimage] ***10***
2001
Photograph
50 x 75 cm
Nordnorsk Kunstmuseum, Tromsø, Norway

Josef Halse
(b. 1951)
Kautokeino, Norway

Untitled
2000
Acrylic on canvas
93 x 80 cm
On loan from Anita Schmid and Peter Rust,
Kautokeino, Norway

Marja Helander
(b. 1965)
Helsinki, Finland

Utsjoki, Finland
2001
Photograph
40 x 47 cm
On loan from Sámi Museum,
De Samiske Samlinger, Karasjok, Norway

Marja Helander
(b. 1965)
Helsinki, Finland

Utsjoki, Finland
2001
Photograph
40 x 48.7 cm
On loan from Sámi Museum,
De Samiske Samlinger, Karasjok, Norway

Marja Helander
(b. 1965)
Helsinki, Finland

Utsjoki, Finland
2001
Photograph
40.2 x 47.7 cm
On loan from Sámi Museum,
De Samiske Samlinger, Karasjok, Norway

Mattiusi Iyaituk

(b. 1950)

Ivujivik, Quebec

Old Qulliq Being Carried by a Woman

2000

Serpentine, marble, caribou antler, musk-ox hair and sinew

63.5 x 31 x 16 cm

Collection of The Winnipeg Art Gallery; acquired with funds from George William Battershill in memory of his wife Helen Battershill and with funds from an anonymous donor

In this sculpture the old *qulliq* or oil lamp—that would have actually been used at one time—becomes the body of the woman who is "carrying" it. This co-joining emphasizes the woman's important role in keeping the oil lamp burning.

Arnold Johansen

(b. 1953)

Hammerfest, Norway

Mats

2001

PVC and steel

150 x 115 cm

On loan from the artist

Arnold Johansen

(b. 1953)

Hammerfest, Norway

Kraakungan

2004

PVC and steel

100 x 147 cm

On loan from the artist

Annelise Josefsen
(b. 1949)
Kokelv, Norway

Lilledama [The Little Lady]
2001
Stone
29.5 x 15 x 20 cm
On loan from Sámi Museum,
De Samiske Samlinger, Karasjok, Norway

Per Isak Juuso
(b. 1953)
Jokkmokk, Sweden

Meavrresgárri [Sacred Drum]
2000
Reindeer skin, wood and reindeer horn
12 x 24 x 34
On loan from Sámi Museum,
De Samiske Samlinger, Karasjok, Norway

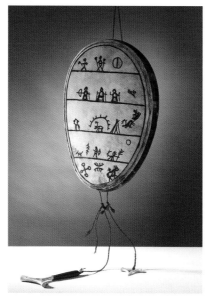

Silas Kayakjuak
(b. 1956)

Hall Beach, Nunavut and Ottawa, Ontario

Drum Dancers

2003

Stone, baleen and ivory

14 x 9 x 8 cm

On loan from John Cowan, Toronto

Silas Kayakjuak
(b. 1956)

Hall Beach, Nunavut and Ottawa, Ontario

Throat Singers

2003

Ivory and stone

5 x 6.5 x 3 cm

On loan from John Cowan, Toronto

Silas Kayakjuak
(b. 1956)

Hall Beach, Nunavut and Ottawa, Ontario

Drum Dancer

2003

Stone, baleen and ivory

17 x 8 x 5.5 cm

On loan from John Cowan, Toronto

Janet Kigusiuq
(1926-2005)
Baker Lake, Nunavut

Pitsiit [Drying Fish]
2001
Paper collage
57.6 x 76.5 cm
On loan from John and Joyce Price, Seattle

Janet Kigusiuq
(1926-2005)
Baker Lake, Nunavut

Arctic Landscape [River with Pebbled Shore]
2002
Pencil crayon
56 x 75.5 cm
On loan from Neil Devitt, Regina

Floyd Kuptana
(b. 1964)

Paulatuk, NWT and Toronto, Ontario

Abductor of Souls

2005

Stone, antler, ivory, leather, hair and mirror

51 x 53.5 x 28 cm

On loan from Sharon and David Frost

The abductor of souls, a hideous old woman who in traditional tales steals the souls of misbehaving children, has been
given a modern makeover by the artist—although he doesn't
seem to have improved her looks.

Floyd Kuptana
(b. 1964)

Paulatuk, NWT and Toronto, Ontario

Patriotic Shaman

2002

Stone, antler, metal and inlay

31 x 39.5 x 20 cm

On loan from Feheley Fine Arts, Toronto

Johanne Losoa Larsson
(b. 1943)
Lillehammer, Norway

Blå natur [Blue Nature]
2003
Oil on canvas
170 x 230 cm
On loan from Sámi Museum,
De Samiske Samlinger, Karasjok, Norway

Max Lundstöm
(b. 1950)
Vilhelmina, Sweden

Black
2004
Birch burl and reindeer horn
14 x 46 x 32 cm diameter
On loan from the artist

Britta Marakatt-Labba
(b. 1951)
Soppero, Sweden

Reindeer Drive
2000
Linen and embroidery thread
53 x 93 cm
On loan from the artist

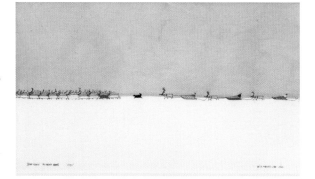

Michael Massie
(b. 1962)

Kippens, Newfoundland and Labrador

Come Sit and Have Some Tea
2005

Anhydrite, sterling silver, ebony and bone

40 x 51.5 x 29 cm (figure), 14 x 28 x 9 cm (teapot)

On loan from Christopher Bredt and
Jamie Cameron, Toronto

"Originally, I wanted to make a piece of a woman holding a teapot—but, after some reflection, I thought it would be more appropriate to make an image of me with a teapot in my hand ... I figured that as I am the one that makes them, it should be me holding one!

"I wanted the figure to be seated, expressing comfort and relaxation—things we associate with the act of taking tea—and the lifted eyebrows, as if to say 'Oooh', I am told, are things that I do. There are certain occasions where people take out their best silverware for company, and I wanted this teapot to be along those lines for this piece. I went back to much earlier designs for the form of the teapot, using the irregular planes as in "tea with Pablo" and "little jimmy", and I used the textured surface rather than a polished surface because I wanted you to see the piece for its form, rather than for how it takes in its surroundings. The pot does refer to the bird teapots through the handles on the lid – and I came up with the rope motif for the handle as it is literally connecting the two pieces together.

I am wearing a parka in this work because I have noticed that every time I have tea outdoors, it always tastes better – and it brings back memories of times up north when I have had students in for tea – and they always wore their coats, no matter how long they stayed!" (Michael Massie in *Tea and a Story with Michael Massie*, Spirit Wrestler Gallery 2005).

Eva Ikinilq Nagyougalik
(b. 1965)

and her daughter

Sophie Kotsik Nagyougalik
(b. 1990)

both Baker Lake, Nunavut

I Love Summer
2005

Wool, felt, and embroidery floss

46 x 72 cm

On loan from John and Joyce Price, Seattle

Hege Annestad Nilsen
(b. 1966)
Hammerfest, Norway

Portrett [Portrait]
2002
Photograph
100 x 100 cm
On loan from Sámi Museum,
De Samiske Samlinger, Karasjok, Norway

Hege Annestad Nilsen
(b. 1966)
Hammerfest, Norway

Portrett [Portrait]
2002
Photograph
100 x 100 cm
On loan from Sámi Museum,
De Samiske Samlinger, Karasjok, Norway

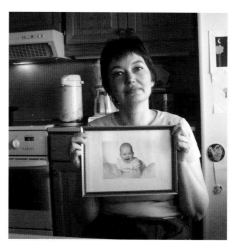

Hege Annestad Nilsen
(b. 1966)
Hammerfest, Norway

Portrett [Portrait]
2002
Photograph
100 x 100 cm
On loan from Sámi Museum,
De Samiske Samlinger, Karasjok, Norway

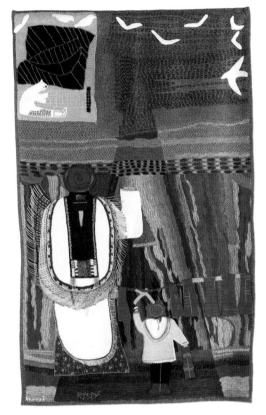

Janet Nungnik
(b. 1954)
Baker Lake, Nunavut

Untitled (On the Land)
2005
Wool, felt, printed cotton, beads, embroidery floss
and thread
146 x 93 cm
On loan from Marion Scott Gallery, Vancouver

Hilde Skancke Pedersen
(b. 1953)

Kautokeino, Norway

Livstegn [Sign of Life] *1*
2003
Photograph and mixed media
61 x 171 cm
On loan from Sámi Museum,
De Samiske Samlinger, Karasjok, Norway

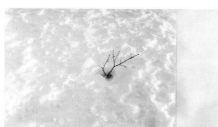

Hilde Skancke Pedersen
(b. 1953)

Kautokeino, Norway

Livstegn [Sign of Life] *2*
2003
Photograph and mixed media
61 x 171 cm
On loan from Sámi Museum,
De Samiske Samlinger, Karasjok, Norway

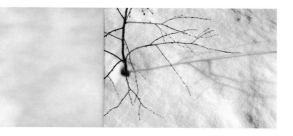

Hilde Skancke Pedersen
(b. 1953)

Kautokeino, Norway

Livstegn [Sign of Life] *4*
2003
Photograph and mixed media
61 x 171 cm
On loan from Sámi Museum,
De Samiske Samlinger, Karasjok, Norway

Hilde Skancke Pedersen
(b. 1953)

Kautokeino, Norway

Livstegn [Sign of Life] *6*
2003
Photograph and mixed media
61 x 171 cm
On loan from Sámi Museum,
De Samiske Samlinger, Karasjok, Norway

Inga Nordsletta Pedersen
(b. 1932)
Karasjok, Norway

Gollegiisa
2002
Wool
100 x 125 cm
On loan from Sámi Museum,
De Samiske Samlinger, Karasjok, Norway

Synnøve Persen
(b. 1950)
Lakselv, Norway

Turning Point
2000
Oil on canvas
150 x 146
On loan from Sámi Museum,
De Samiske Samlinger, Karasjok, Norway

Outi Pieski
(b. 1973)
Numminen, Finland

Kveldshimmel/Eahkedisalbmi [Evening Sky]
2001
Acrylic on textile
150 x 150 cm
On loan from Sámi Museum,
De Samiske Samlinger, Karasjok, Norway

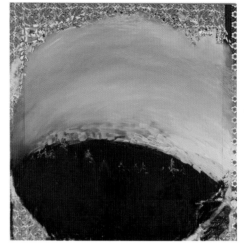

Jamasie Pudloo Pitseolak
(b. 1968)
Cape Dorset, Nunavut

Domestic Sewing Machine
2005
Stone and ivory
11.5 x 15 x 6 cm
On loan from John and Joyce Price, Seattle

Annie Pootoogook
(b. 1969)
Cape Dorset, Nunavut

Christmas Games at the Community Hall
2000/2001
Pencil, ink and pencil crayon
33 x 51 cm
On loan from Feheley Fine Arts, Toronto

Annie Pootoogook
(b. 1969)
Cape Dorset, Nunavut

Three Generations of Women Artists
2003
Pencil, ink and pencil crayon
66 x 51 cm
On loan from John and Joyce Price, Seattle

Annie Pootoogook
(b. 1969)
Cape Dorset, Nunavut

Playing Super Nintendo
2003/2004
Pencil crayon and ink
51 x 66 cm
On loan from the Art Gallery of Hamilton, Hamilton

Kananginak Pootoogook

(b. 1935)

Cape Dorset, Nunavut

White Man Filming Inuk Drumming

2002

Pencil crayon and ink

51 x 66 cm

On loan from John and Joyce Price, Seattle

The artist has written on the drawing: "Some white people were awed by what they had never seen before, especially the traditional Inuit way of life."

Kananginak Pootoogook

(b. 1935)

Cape Dorset, Nunavut

Amiraijaqtuq: Shedding the Velvet

2004

Stonecut and stencil printed by

Kavavow Mannomee (b. 1958)

43.7 x 38.3

On loan from Dorset Fine Arts, Toronto

Napachie Pootoogook

(1938-2002)

Cape Dorset, Nunavut

Winsome Travellers

2002

Etching and aquatint printed by

Studio PM, Montreal

80.4 x 82.8 cm

On loan from Dorset Fine Arts, Toronto

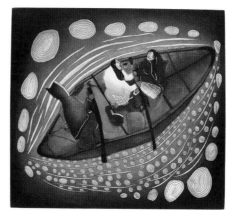

Palaya Qiatsuq

(b. 1965)
Cape Dorset, Nunavut

Sedna

2002
Marble and sepentine
20 x 40 x 9 cm
On loan from Dorset Fine Arts, Toronto

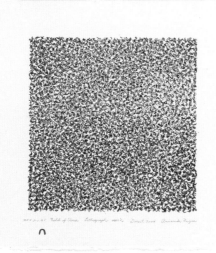

Anirnik Ragee

(b. 1935)
Cape Dorset, Nunavut

Field of Verse

2004
Lithograph printed by Pitseolak Niviaqsi (b. 1947)
36 x 35.8 cm
On loan from Dorset Fine Arts, Toronto

The random words arranged across the surface of this
print were written with the syllabic symbols used in writing
the Inuktitut language by the artist—in her sixties but a
new comer to the print studios—working directly on the
lithographic stone.

Abraham Anghik Ruben
(b. 1951)
Paulatuk, NWT and Salt Spring Island, British Columbia

Kittigazuit
1999-2000
Whalebone, Brazilian soapstone and African wonderstone
129.5 x 42.5 x 73 cm
Collection of The Winnipeg Art Gallery; Commissioned from
the artist; Acquired with funds from The Winnipeg Art Gallery
Foundation Inc. and with the support of The Canada Council
for the Arts Acquisition Assistance Program

"Kittigazuit was once a large and flourishing settlement located on the ocean coastline southwest of Tuktoyaktuk in the Mackenzie Delta area. It flourished in the 19th century because of plentiful fishing, whaling and hunting. However, a series of epidemics of scarlet fever, measles, and influenza from 1865 to 1902 killed many of its inhabitants, including members of the artist's family. Survivors left the community and dispersed along the coastline, and today it is little more than a landmark on the tundra.

"*Kittigazuit* is made from an ancient piece of whalebone that was part of the skull of a bowhead whale. At the base of the carving, there are a number of human faces that have no eyes, symbolizing the people who died in the epidemic. They are roughly carved in the porous bone to give a sense of history, indicating that this happened a long time ago. The sculpture has animals clustered around it: loons, seals, ravens, and bears. A raven's head beside the full moon signifies that, unlike the people, the animals continued on. There is an open space in the skull, signifying an empty land where people used to live. A woman's *amautik* (parka) is empty of children, just as the land is empty of people.

Not only a generation, but also a culture has been lost,
as Mackenzie Inuit culture changed with the arrival of many people from Alaska"
(Darlene Coward Wight in *Abraham Anghik Ruben*, The Winnipeg Art Gallery 2001).

Alf Magne Salo
(b. 1959)
Samuelsberg, Norway

Apsis 3
2001
Acrylic on canvas
170 x 240 cm
On loan from Sámi Museum,
De Samiske Samlinger, Karasjok, Norway

Iria Čiekča Schmidt

(b. 1941)
Tammisaari, Finland

Leaibolmmái/Jaktgudinnen [The Goddess of Hunting]
2000
collage
90 x 64 cm
On loan from Sámi Museum,
De Samiske Samlinger, Karasjok, Norway

Toonoo Sharky

(b. 1970)
Cape Dorset, Nunavut

Drum Dancers
2000
Mixed media
20 x 17 x 19 cm
On loan from Christopher Bredt and Jamie Cameron,
Toronto

Nick Sikkuark
(b. 1943)
Pelly Bay, Nunavut

Untitled (Hunter Carrying Caribou Head)
2002
Whalebone, caribou antler, caribou skull,
sinew and caribou fur
44.5 x 25 x 42.5 cm
On loan from John and Joyce Price, Seattle

Nick Sikkuark
(b. 1943)
Pelly Bay, Nunavut

Imagining Things
2003
Pencil crayon
35.5 x 40.5 cm
On loan from John and Joyce Price, Seattle

"Sometimes, somewhere, anywhere, we see things that look
like a person, or objects resembling things ... images in the
land, mountains, ice ridges, sea ice, or rocks"
(Nick Sikkuark in Robert Kardosh *The Art of Nick Sikkuark*,
Marion Scott Gallery 2003).

Nick Sikkuark
(b. 1943)
Pelly Bay, Nunavut

Untitled (Flying Shaman Heads)
2003
Pencil crayon
34 x 28 cm
On loan from John and Joyce Price, Seattle

Nick Sikkuark
(b. 1943)
Pelly Bay, Nunavut

Untitled (Landscape Fragments)
2003
Pencil crayon
28 x 34 cm
On loan from John and Joyce Price, Seattle

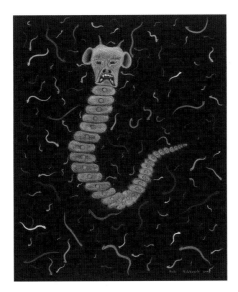

Nick Sikkuark
(b. 1943)
Pelly Bay, Nunavut

Untitled (Worm Spirit)
2003
Pencil crayon
34 x 28 cm
On loan from John and Joyce Price, Seattle

Annie Taipanak

(b. 1931)
Baker Lake, Nunavut

Untitled (Life on the Land)
2004
Wool, felt and embroidery floss
198 x 134.5 cm
On loan from Marion Scott Gallery, Vancouver

Jutai Toonoo

(b. 1959)
Cape Dorset, Nunavut

A Great Man [Osuitok Ipeelee]
2001
Stone
53 x 30.5 x 16 cm
On loan from John and Joyce Price, Seattle

"I was at camp with Osuitok and he wasn't the same
man I used to know. This is an image of what he
used to be. He was a great man; he still is"
(Jutai Toonoo, *Toonoo's Legacy*, Feheley Fine Arts, 2002).

Osuitok Ipeelee (b. 1923), an internationally known
sculptor from Cape Dorset, is an elder now
and does little carving.

Oviloo Tunnillie

(b. 1949)

Cape Dorset, Nunavut and Montreal, Québec

Untitled (Self-portrait)

2000

Stone

19 x 11.5 x 18 cm

On loan from Judy Kardosh, Vancouver

Oviloo Tunnillie

(b. 1949)

Cape Dorset, Nunavut and Montreal, Québec

Oviloo and Her Daughter Tye with Photograph

2002

Stone

35.5 x 29 x 16.5 cm

On loan from John and Joyce Price, Seattle

Oviloo and her daughter Tye are looking at a photograph taken of them by Jerry Riley in 1990 when Tye was a child.

Ingunn Utsi
(b. 1948)
Repvåg, Norway

Den med gittervindu og drømmer om frihet
[The One with a Lattice Window and Dreams of Freedom]
2004
Wood (Pasvik pine from northeast Norway),
stones, glass, amber and feathers
280 cm
On loan from Honningsvåg Fiskarfagskole,
og videregående skole, Nordkapp

Nils Arvid Westerfjell
(b. 1961)
Namsskogan, Norway

Guadtasdahke / Beltering [Woman's Sewing Kit]
2002
Reindeer skin, horn and sinew, brass,
cloth and beads
33 x 40 cm (approximate)
On loan from Sámi Museum,
De Samiske Samlinger, Karasjok, Norway

ACKNOWLEDGEMENTS

My first thanks rightly belong to Shirley Madill of the Art Gallery of Hamilton who asked me to act as curator of this exhibition; it was her commitment that overcame my original misgivings about an exhibition whose sole curatorial concept seemed to be that it combined Sámi and Inuit art. Secondly I would like to express my appreciation to Pat Feheley, who was involved with this project at the very beginning, for sharing her resources and research material with me. My learning curve on contemporary Sámi art was a steep one and I could not have managed without Irene Snarby, Curator at the Sámi Museum in Karasjok, Norway. Irene was very generous with her time, knowledge and guidance and also served as a congenial host and guide. I would also like to thank Hilde Skancke Pedersen for showing me around Kautokeino. My meetings, visits to galleries and appointments in Norway were all arranged by Bjørn Petter Hernes, Public Affairs Officer at the Canadian Embassy in Oslo, with the assistance of Åsta Rosenberg; I am truly grateful for their efficiency and kindness.

Since the intention of this exhibition was to include works made between 2000 and 2005, many were borrowed directly from commercial galleries, collectors and the artists themselves. This meant collectors parting with new found treasures and galleries and artists lending works that could otherwise be sold. I would especially like to acknowledge all the artists included here; their work has made this an exciting, visually pleasing and unusual exhibition.

Finally, a note of thanks to the staff of the Art Gallery of Hamilton—with special appreciation to Kathryn Rumbold—for making all the arrangements for the exhibition, its installation and tour.

Jean Blodgett, *Guest Curator*

AGH Staff

LOUISE DOMPIERRE
President & C.E.O.

ARLENE M. LEE
Executive Assistant

KATHRYN RUMBOLD
Director of Programmes

TOBI BRUCE
Senior Curator/
Curator, Historical Art

PATRICK SHAW CABLE
Curator of European Art

SARA KNELMAN
Curator of Contemporary Art

CHRISTINE BRAUN
Registrar

GREG DAWE
Chief Preparator

PAULA ESTEVES MAURO
Preparator

ROD DEMERLING
Preparator

RAND ANDERSON
Contract Preparator

LAURIE KILGOUR
Educator

THEA DEMETRAKOPOULOS
Media Programming

ADRIAN EMBERLEY
Library Archivist

HELEN HADDEN
Volunteer Librarian

MARGARET HAYES
Director,
Finance & Administration

SHARADA SEEMALA
Officer, Finance &
Administration

JULIE SMITH
Database Coordinator

LARISSA CIUPKA
Director, Marketing &
Communications

STEVE DENYES
Manager, Communications

VINCE FRANCO
Manager, Marketing

JANINE BELZAK
Manager, Hospitality Services

ANNETTE PAIEMENT
Manager, Special Events &
Corporate Services

TINA EIDUKAITIS
Manager, Membership

JAMES GIRT
Visitor Services Coordinator

CAROLE GARDINER
Director, Retail Operations

KATHRYN FABBRICINO
Retail Associate

ROBERT MARENTETTE
Director, Security &
Building Manager

CARLOS BRIEIRO
Building Manager

SHIRLEY MADILL
Vice-President and C.O.O.
(former)

BIBLIOGRAPHY

Ájtte - Swedish Mountain and Sámi Museum. 1993. The Sámi: People of the Sun and Wind. Translated by Thomas Rutschman. Jokkmokk: Ájtte - Swedish Mountain and Sámi Museum.

Ayre, Robert. 1993. "Carving is Healing to Me: An Interview with Manasie Akpaliapik." Inuit Art Quarterly 8:4.

Bergsmo, Trym Ivar. 2001. Boazojahki: Four Seasons with the Reindeer People. English text by Carol B. Edkman. Oslo: Pantagruel Forlag AS.

Bjørklund, Ivar. 2000. Sápmi – Becoming a Nation: The Emergence of a Sámi National Community. Tromsø: Tromsø Museum.

Blodgett, Jean. 2006. Curatorial Notes: "In the Shadow of the Midnight Sun: Sámi and Inuit Art: 2000-2005." Inuit Art Quarterly 21:3.

_____. 1999. Three Women, Three Generations. Kleinburg: McMichael Canadian Art Collection.

Conrad, Jo Ann. 1999. Contested Terrain: Land, Language, and Lore in Contemporary Sámi Politics. Ph.D. dissertation. Ann Arbor: UMI Microform 9931220.

Feheley, Patricia M. 2004. "Modern Language: The Art of Annie Pootoogook." Inuit Art Quarterly 19:2.

Feheley Fine Arts. 2002a. Recent Works on Paper by Janet Kigusiuq. Toronto: Feheley Fine Arts.

_____. 2002b. Toonoo's Legacy: Oviloo Tunnillie, Jutai Toonoo, Sam Toonoo and Sheojuke Toonoo. Toronto: Feheley Fine Arts.

_____. 2003a. Catching the Eye: Sculpture by Isaci Etidloie. Toronto: Feheley Fine Arts.

_____. 2003b. Works on Paper by Annie Pootoogook. Toronto: Feheley Fine Arts.

_____. 2004. Kenojuak and Onward: Arnaqu Ashevak, Adamie Ashevak, Kenojuak Ashevak. Toronto: Feheley Fine Arts.

_____. 2005. Windows on Kinngait: The Drawings of Napachie Pootoogook and Annie Pootoogook. Toronto: Feheley Fine Arts.

Fox, Matthew. 1996. "Mike Massie of Labrador." Inuit Art Quarterly 11:1.

_____. 2001a. "Padlaya Qiatsuk: Encouraging Young Carvers to Persevere." Inuit Art Quarterly 16:1.

_____. 2001b. "Focus on Jutai Toonoo, Contemporary Carver." Inuit Art Quarterly 16:4.

Gaski, Harald, editor. 1996. In the Shadow of the Midnight Sun: Contemporary Sámi Prose and Poetry. Karasjok: Davvi Girji.

_____. 1997. Sámi Culture in a New Era: The Norwegian Sámi Experience. Karasjok: Davvi Girji.

Grunder, Ursula. 2004. "Manasie Akpaliapik: Between the Spiritual and Material." Inuit Art Quarterly 19:3 & 4.

Gunderson, Sonia. 2004. "Michael Massie: Playing in His Own World." Inuit Art Quarterly 19:3 & 4.

Gustavison, Susan. 1999. Northern Rock: Contemporary Inuit Stone Sculpture. Kleinburg: McMichael Canadian Art Collection.

Hætta, Odd Mathis. 1993. Sámi: An Indigenous People of the Arctic. Karasjok: Davvi Girji.

Helander, Elina, editor. 1996. Awakened Voices: The Return of Sámi Knowledge. Kautokeino: Nordic Sámi Institute.

Helander, Elina and Kaarina Kailo, editors. 1998. No Beginning, No End: Sámi Speak Up. Edmonton, Alberta: Canadian Circumpolar Institute in cooperation with the Nordic Sámi Institute, Finland.

Inuit Art Quarterly. 1993 (8:3). Cover image.

_____. 2004 (19:3 & 4). "Kananginak Pootoogook."

_____. 2004 (19:3 & 4). "Silas Kayakjuak."

Iyaituk, Mattiusi. 2001. "Inuit Art from a Sculptor's Perspective." Inuit Art Quarterly 16:4.

Kardosh, Robert. 1994. Oviloo Tunnillie. Vancouver: Marion Scott Gallery.

_____. 2003. The Art of Nick Sikkuark: Sculpture & Drawings. Vancouver: Marion Scott Gallery.

_____. 2005a. "Natural Fantasia: The Wonderful World of Nick Sikkuark (Part I)." Inuit Art Quarterly 20:1.

_____. 2005b. "Natural Fantasia: The Wonderful World of Nick Sikkuark (Part II)." Inuit Art Quarterly 20:2.